12/20 ⑧ u/o 10/19

D0392218

After Europe

After Europe

Ivan Krastev

PENN

UNIVERSITY OF PENNSYLVANIA PRESS

PHILADELPHIA

Copyright © 2017 University of Pennsylvania Press

All rights reserved. Except for brief quotations used for purposes of review or scholarly citation, none of this book may be reproduced in any form by any means without written permission from the publisher.

Published by
University of Pennsylvania Press
Philadelphia, Pennsylvania 19104-4112
www.upenn.edu/pennpress

Printed in the United States of America

A Cataloging-in-Publication record is available
from the Library of Congress

Cover design by John Hubbard

ISBN 978-0-8122-4943-9 hardcover
ISBN 978-0-8122-9426-2 ebook

Contents

The Déjà Vu Mind-Set

On one of the last days of June 1914, a telegram arrived in a remote garrison town on the border of the Habsburg Empire. The telegram consisted of a single sentence printed in capital letters: "HEIR TO THE THRONE RUMORED ASSASSINATED IN SARAJEVO." In a moment of disbelief, one of the emperor's officers, Count Battyanyi, began inexplicably speaking in his native Hungarian to his compatriots about the death of Archduke Franz Ferdinand, a man who had been perceived as partial to the Slavs. Lieutenant Jelacich, a Slovene who felt uneasy about Hungarians—especially because of their suspected disloyalty to the throne—insisted that the conversation be held in the more customary German. "Then I will say it in German," Count Battyanyi assented. "We are in agreement, my countrymen and I: We can be glad the bastard is gone."

This was the end of the multiethnic Habsburg Empire—at least the way Joseph Roth captured it in his magisterial novel *The Radetzky March.*[1] The empire's final demise was partly fate, partly murder, partly suicide, and partly just sheer bad luck. While historians disagree whether the empire's collapse was a natural death caused by institutional exhaustion or a violent murder at the hands of World War I, the ghost of the failed Habsburg experiment continues to haunt European minds. Oscar Jaszi—witness to (and historian of) the end of the monarchy—was spot-on in 1929 when he wrote that "if the Austro-Hungarian state experiment had been really successful, the Habsburg monarchy would have solved on its territory the most fundamental problem of present Europe. . . . How it is possible to unite national individualities of divergent ideals and traditions in such a way that each of them can continue its own particular life, while at the same time limiting its national sovereignty enough to make peaceful and effective international cooperation possible?"[2]

As we know, the experiment never came to a definitive conclusion, because Europe failed to resolve its thorniest problem. Roth's story is a powerful testament that when man-made worlds of political and cultural artifice disappear, they do so quickly. The end is both a natural outcome of structural deficiencies and the equivalent of a traffic accident—an unintended consequence, say, or an act of sleepwalking, a particular moment that has a dynamic all of its own. It is both inevitable and inadvertent.

Are we experiencing a similar "disintegration moment" in Europe today? Do both Britain's democratic decision to leave the union (in economic terms, it is the equivalent of the egress of twenty smaller EU member countries) and the rise of Euroskeptic parties on the continent signal the unraveling of our latter-day experiment in resolving Europe's most fundamental problem? Is the European Union doomed to fall apart in the fashion of the Habsburg Empire? Is 2017—marked by critical elections in the Netherlands, France, and Germany—fated to be as momentous a year as 1917?

Jan Zielonka has aptly observed that "we have many theories of European integration, but practically none of European disintegration."[3] This is not accidental. The architects of the European project have fooled themselves into believing that avoiding mentioning the "D" word is a surefire way to prevent it from happening. For them, European integration was like a speed train—never stop and never look back. Making the European Union's disintegration unthinkable was the preferred strategy over making integration irreversible. But there are two other reasons for the dearth of theories on disintegration. First is the problem of definition: How can disintegration be distinguished from reform or reconfiguration of the union? Would the departure of a group of countries from the eurozone, or from the union itself, amount to disintegration? Or would the decline of the EU's global influence and the reversal of some major achievements of European integration (such as the free movement of people or the abolition of institutions like the Court of Justice of the European Union) be evidence of disintegration? Does the emergence of a two-tier EU amount to disintegration, or is it just a step toward a closer and more perfect union? Might it be possible for a union populated by illiberal democracies to continue the same political project?

Then there's the irony that at the very moment when political leaders and the general public are paralyzed by a fear of disintegration, Europe is more integrated than ever before. The financial crisis made the idea of a banking union a reality. The need for an effective response to the rise in terrorist threats has compelled Europeans to cooperate—more than ever before—in the field of security. And what is most paradoxical, the multiple crises currently faced by the union make ordinary Germans unusually interested in the problems of the Greek and Italian economies and press Poles and Hungarians to be attentive to Germany's asylum policies. Europeans live in fear of disintegration while the union looks more than ever like a community of fate.

Imagining European disintegration has hardly been in vogue with fiction writers either. There are scores of novels that ask what would have happened if Nazi Germany had triumphed in World War II. We likewise have fantasies of what could have transpired if the Soviets had won the Cold War—or, for that matter, if the communist revolution had taken place in New York instead of Petrograd. But almost nobody has been particularly inspired to narrate the fictional story of the European Union's disintegration. The sole exception is, perhaps, José Saramago. In his novel, *The Stone Raft*, a river that flows from France to Spain disappears into the ground and the entire Iberian Peninsula breaks off from Europe and heads west across the Atlantic.[4]

George Orwell was certainly right to suggest that "to see what is in front of one's nose needs a constant struggle." On January 1, 1992, the world woke up to learn that the Soviet Union was no longer on the map. One of the world's two superpowers had collapsed without a war, an alien invasion, or any other catastrophe, with the exception of one farcical, unsuccessful coup. The collapse happened contrary to every expectation that the Soviet empire was too big to fail, too stable to collapse, and too nuked-up to be defeated and had survived too much turbulence to simply implode. As late as 1990, a group of leading American experts insisted that "sensationalist scenarios make for exciting reading but . . . in the real world various stabilizers and retarding factors exist; societies frequently undergo crises, even grave and dangerous ones, but they seldom commit suicide."[5] But in reality, societies sometimes *do* commit suicide, and they do it with a certain élan as well.

As it was a century ago, Europeans today are living at a moment when paralyzing uncertainty captures a society's imagination. It is a moment when political leaders and ordinary citizens alike are torn between hectic activity and fatalistic passivity, a moment when what was until now *unthinkable*—the disintegration of the union—begins to be perceived as *inevitable*. And it is a moment when the narratives and assumptions that only yesterday guided our actions begin to seem not only outdated but nearly unintelligible. As we know from history, the fact that something appears absurd and irrational hardly means it can't happen. And the ever-present Central European nostalgia for the liberal Habsburgs is the best proof that sometimes we are able to appreciate something only after it is gone.

The European Union has always been an idea in search of a reality. But there is a growing worry that what once kept the union together no longer holds. Shared memories of the Second World War, for example, have faded from view: half of all fifteen- and sixteen-year-olds in German high schools don't even know that Hitler was a dictator, while a third believe that he protected human rights. As Timur Vermes's 2011 satirical novel *Look Who's Back* suggests, the question is no longer whether it's possible for Hitler to come back; it's whether we'd even be able to recognize him. The novel sold more than a million copies in Germany. "The end of history" that Francis Fukuyama promised us in 1989 may well have arrived, but in the perverse sense that historical experience no longer matters and few are really interested in it.[6]

The geopolitical rationale for European unity vanished with the Soviet Union's collapse. And Putin's Russia, threatening as it may be, cannot fill this existential void. Europeans today are more insecure than in the waning days of the Cold War. Surveys indicate that the majority of Britons, Germans, and French believe that the world is heading to a major war, but the external threats that the EU faces divide rather than unify the continent. A recent survey conducted by Gallup International shows that in a case of a major security crisis, the public in at least three of the EU member states (Bulgaria, Greece, and Slovenia) would look to Russia and not to the West for assistance. The nature of the transatlantic relationship has also changed dramatically. Donald Trump is the first American president who does not believe that the preservation of the European Union should be a strategic objective of US foreign policy.

The welfare state, once the heart of the postwar political consensus, has also come under question. Europe is aging—the median age on the continent is expected to increase to 52.3 years in 2050 from 37.7 years in 2003—and the future of European prosperity can hardly be taken for granted. Most Europeans believe that the lives of today's children will be more difficult than those of their own generation; and as the refugee crisis demonstrates, immigration is unlikely to provide Europe with a solution for its demographic weakness.

But it is not only demography that puts the European welfare state in a precarious position. According to Wolfgang Streeck, the director of the Max Plank Institute and one of Germany's leading sociologists, the European welfare state model has been in crisis since the 1970s. Capitalism has successfully wrested free from the institutions and regulations imposed on it after World War II, and as a result, the much praised European "tax state" has effectively been transformed into a "debt state." Instead of distributing tax revenue from the rich to the poor, European governments now maintain their financial health by borrowing from future generations in the form of deficit spending. The result is that democratic voters have lost the power to regulate the market and therefore undermined the very foundations of the postwar welfare state.

Finally, the European Union has been cursed by a change in ideological fashions. In 2014, the EU was diagnosed with what might be called an "autistic disorder." The diagnosis came as a surprise, but the symptoms were impossible to miss: impairment in social interaction, weakening of communication skills, restricted interests, and repetitive behavior. The union manifested a lack of intuition about others that many people once had taken for granted. This was particularly clear during the Ukrainian crisis when, for a long time, the EU pretended that Russia wouldn't protest Kiev joining the EU and was then flummoxed when Putin deployed force to annex Crimea. It also cropped up in Brussels's repeated claim that the alienation of citizens from the European project was simply the result of ineffective communication. In the wake of the Ukrainian crisis, after talking on the phone with Russian president Vladimir Putin, German chancellor Angela Merkel came to the conclusion that he was living in "another world." Three years later, the question is, which of the two is living in the "real world"?

After the end of the Cold War and the expansion of the union, Brussels fell head over heels for its social and political model, adopting a highly uncritical view of the direction world history was heading. European public opinion had assumed that globalization would hasten the decline of states as key international actors and nationalism as a core political motivator. Europeans interpreted their own post-WWII experience of overcoming ethnic nationalism and political theology as a signal of a universal trend. As Mark Leonard put it in his aspirational book *Why Europe Will Run the 21st Century*, "Europe represents a synthesis of the energy and freedom that come from liberalism with the stability and welfare that come from social democracy. As the world becomes richer and moves beyond satisfying basic needs such as hunger and health, the European way of life will become irresistible."[7] But what just yesterday seemed universally applicable has now begun to look exceptional. A passing glance at China, India, and Russia, not to speak of the vast reaches of the Muslim world, makes clear that both ethnic nationalism and religion remain major driving forces in global politics. Europe's postmodernism, postnationalism, and secularism make it different from the rest of the world, not a harbinger of what necessarily awaits it. What is also visible in the context of the refugee crisis is that national loyalties, once considered dead and buried, are back—with a vengeance—in contemporary Europe.

In recent years, Europeans have come to realize that although the EU's political model is admirable, it is unlikely to become universal or even spread to its immediate neighbors. This is a European version of the "Galapagos Syndrome" experienced by Japanese technology companies. A few years ago, these companies became aware that although Japan made the best 3G phones in the world, they could not find a global market because the rest of the world could not catch up with the technological innovations to use these "perfect" devices. Rather than being too big to fail, Japan's phones, developed in protected isolation from the challenges of the outside world, had become too perfect to succeed. Now it is Europe that is facing its own "Galapagos" moment.[8] It may be that Europe's postmodern order has become so advanced and particular to its environment that it is impossible for others to follow.

It is this new reality that first inspired me to think in terms of *after Europe*. *After Europe* signifies that the old continent has both lost its centrality in global politics and the confidence of Europeans themselves—the confidence that its political choices can shape the future of the world. *After Europe* means that the European project has lost its teleological appeal and that the idea of a "United States of Europe" is less inspiring than at perhaps any other moment in the last fifty years. *After Europe* means that Europe is suffering from an identity crisis in which its Christian and Enlightenment legacies are no longer secure. *After Europe* does not necessarily mean that the European Union is at an end so much as it signals that we need to leave behind our naïve hopes and expectations about the future shape of Europe and the world.

The following is a reflection on the fate of Europe in the style of Antonio Gramsci's "pessimism of the intellect, optimism of the will." I am someone who believes that the disintegration train has left Brussels's station—and who fears it will doom the continent to disarray and global irrelevance. It will likely transform a sympathetic environment of tolerance and openness to one characterized by a bullying narrow-mindedness. It may cause the breakdown of liberal democracies on Europe's periphery and usher in the collapse of several existing member states. It will not necessarily lead to war, but it will probably contribute to misery and turmoil. Political, cultural, and economic cooperation won't evaporate, but the dream of a Europe free and united probably will.

At the same time, I believe that in order to regain legitimacy there is no need for the European Union to solve all the problems it faces. What is necessary is that five years from now Europeans are capable of traveling freely in Europe, the euro is on track to survive as the common currency of at least some of the member states, and citizens are able both to elect their governments freely and to sue them in Strasbourg's European Court of Human Rights. "Who speaks of victory?" asks the great German poet Rainer Maria Rilke. "To endure is all." But even enduring will not be easy.

If the union collapses, the logic of its fragmentation will be that of a bank run and not of a revolution. The EU's implosion does not have to result from a victory of "exiters" over "remainers" in state referenda; it will more likely be an unintended consequence of the union's long-term dysfunction (or perceived dysfunction), compounded by a misreading by elites of national political dynamics. In their fear that the union will fall apart and in a desire to hedge against such an outcome, many European leaders and governments will take actions that make the collapse of the European project a foregone conclusion. And if disintegration does happen, it will be not because the periphery has run away but because the center (Germany, France) has revolted.

The ambition of this book is neither to save the EU nor to mourn it. It is not another tract on the etiology of the European crisis or a pamphlet against the corruption and impotence of European elites. And it is by no means the book of a Euroskeptic. It is simply a meditation on something that will now likely come to pass and an analysis of how our personal experiences of radical historical change shape our present actions. What fascinates me is the political power of what I consider the "déjà vu mind-set"— a condition of feeling haunted by the conviction that what we are experiencing today is a repetition of some previous historical moment or episode.

In this sense, Europe is divided not only between Left and Right, north and south, large and small states, and those who want more Europe and those who want less (or no Europe at all) but also between those who have experienced disintegration firsthand and those who know it only from textbooks. This is the split separating people who endured firsthand the collapse of communism and the disintegration of the once powerful communist bloc and those Westerners who emerged unscathed by any those traumatic events.

It is experience itself that defines the vastly different readings of today's European crisis, whether from

Budapest or from Paris. Eastern Europeans interpret the state of things swept up by a feeling of anxiety, even dread, while western Europeans insist on believing that everything will work out fine. "At the beginning of December 1937 in France," writes the historian Benjamin F. Martin, "if you closed your eyes and wished hard enough, you could almost believe that everything was all right—or at least not any worse than it had been."[9] At the start of 2017, if you close your eyes and wish hard enough, you might believe the same. But because of the personal experience of eastern Europeans—and I am one—shutting one's eyes and believing that everything will be fine is a far more tenuous proposition.

This book might be read as the musings of a mind caught in a déjà vu mind-set. I was in my final year of studying philosophy at Sofia University in 1989 when the world turned upside down. As Andrei Makarevich, the Russian songwriter and underground musician has tellingly put it, "It had never occurred to me that in the Soviet Union anything could ever change. Let alone that it could disappear."[10] Living in communist Bulgaria, I felt the same. The experience of the sudden and nonviolent end of something that we were confident was permanent (until it was no more) is the defining experience in the life of my generation. We were overwhelmed by the opportunities that were suddenly opened up and the newly discovered sense of personal freedom. But we were struck as well by the newly discovered sense of the fragility of all things political.

Living through a great disruption teaches you several lessons. The most important is that what defines the direction of history is sometimes a chain of minor events amid a background of big ideas. As the historian Mary Elise Sarotte argues in her book *Collapse*, the actual opening of the Berlin Wall on the night of November 9, 1989, "was not the result of a decision by political leaders in East Berlin, . . . or of an agreement with the government of West Germany. . . . [It] was not the result of a plan by the four powers that still held ultimate legal authority in divided Berlin. . . . The opening represented a dramatic instance of surprise, a moment when structures both literal and figurative crumbled unexpectedly. A series of accidents, some of them mistakes so minor that they might otherwise have been trivialities."[11] The end of communism is thus less effectively explained by Francis Fukuyama's narrative of "the end of history" than it is by Harold Macmillan's "events, my dear boy, events."

It is the experience of the Soviet collapse that in myriad aspects defines the way eastern Europeans perceive what is taking place today. Witnessing the political turmoil in Europe, we have a sinking feeling that we have been through this before—the only difference being that then it was their world that collapsed. Now it is ours.

It is commonplace in Europe today either to discuss the crisis of the union in terms of the fundamental flaws in its institutional architecture (e.g., the introduction of a common currency in the absence of a common fiscal policy) or to interpret it as an outcome of the EU's democratic deficit. My analysis parts ways with these lines of argument. In my reading, the only way to deal with the risk of disintegration is to recognize clearheadedly that the refugee crisis has dramatically changed the nature of democratic politics on the national level and that what we are witnessing in Europe is not simply a populist riot against the establishment but a voters' rebellion against the meritocratic elites (best symbolized by hard-working, competent officials in Brussels who are nonetheless out of touch with the societies they are supposed to represent and serve). How the refugee crisis has changed European societies and why citizens resent the meritocratic elites are the two issues this book will try to address. (What the refugee crisis has clarified is that Europeans no longer dream of some distant utopia. There really is no imagined perfect land where they want to live. The new dream is for what one might call Nativia—a distant island to which unwanted foreigners can be sent without the slightest pang of guilt.)

This is also a book about revolution. In the twenty-first century, migration is the new revolution—not a twentieth-century revolution of the masses, but an exit-driven revolution of individuals and families. It is inspired not by ideologically inscribed paintings of radiant futures but by Google Maps photos of life on the other side (of the border). In order to succeed, this new revolution doesn't require ideology, political movements, or political leaders. For so many of the wretched of the earth, crossing the European Union's border is a matter of human necessity and hardly a question of a utopian future.

For a growing number of people, the idea of change signifies changing one's country, not one's government. The problem with the migration revolution—as in any revolution, really—is that it contains within itself the capacity to inspire counterrevolution. In this case, the revolution has inspired the rise of threatened majorities as a major force in European politics. These anxious majorities fear that foreigners are taking over their countries and jeopardizing their way of life, and they are convinced that the current crisis is brought on by a conspiracy between cosmopolitan-minded elites and tribal-minded immigrants.

In the age of migration, democracy has begun to operate as an instrument of exclusion, not of inclusion. The key characteristic of many of the right-wing populist parties in Europe is not that they are national-conservative but that they are reactionary. And as Mark Lilla has observed, "The enduring vitality of the reactionary spirit even in the absence of a revolutionary political program" comes from the feeling that to "live a modern life anywhere in the world today, subject to perpetual social and technological changes, is to experience the psychological equivalent of permanent revolution."[12] And for the reactionaries, "The only sane response to apocalypse is to provoke another, in hopes of starting over."

We the Europeans

In his great novel *Death with Interruptions* (2005), José Saramago imagines a society where people live so long that death is deprived of its existential role.[1] At the outset of the new reality, most people are overwhelmed by a sense of euphoria that their lives will be extended. But soon enough, an awkwardness—metaphysical, political, and practical—takes hold. Different institutions question the benefits of a longer life. The Catholic Church worries that "without death there is no resurrection, and without resurrection there is no church." For insurance companies, life without death means the decimation of insurance policies. The state faces the impossible financial task of paying pensions forever. Families with elderly and infirm relatives understand that only death saves them from an eternity of nursing care. The prime minister warns the monarch, "If we don't start dying again, we have no future." Soon enough, a mafia-style cabal emerges to smuggle old and sick people to neighboring countries to die (since death is still an option elsewhere).

Chapter 1

Europe's experience with a world without borders—what we speak of as globalization—resembles Saramago's imagined flirtation with immortality. It is a tale of a sublime dream turned nightmarish. The immediate post-1989 excitement prompted by the shattering of walls has been replaced by a dizzying anxiety and a demand to build fences. Since the Berlin Wall fell—an event heralded as a world opened up—Europe has put up, or started to erect, 1,200 kilometers of fences expressly designed to keep others out.

If only yesterday most Europeans were hopeful about the impact of globalization on their lives, today they are unsettled by a future globalized world. Recent surveys reveal that a majority of Europeans believe that their children will have a tougher life than their own and are convinced that their countries are heading in a wrong direction.

The tourist and the refugee have become symbols of globalization's contrasting faces. The tourist is the protagonist of globalization, appreciated and welcomed with open arms. She is the benevolent foreigner. She comes, spends, smiles, admires, and leaves. She makes us feel connected to a larger world without imposing its problems on us.

By contrast, the refugee (who could have been yesterday's tourist) is the symbol of globalization's threatening nature. He comes weighed down by the misery and trouble of the wider world. He is *among* us, but he is not *of* us. The priority of, for example, the Greek government is to keep refugees far away from tourist destinations. Attracting tourists and rejecting migrants is the short version of Europe's desired world order.

18

In the nineteenth century, European high society embraced the quadrille, a dance in which participants continuously changed partners and roles. The quadrille's intense popularity soon led to its metaphorical usage, with newspaper articles discussing the "stately quadrille"—implying freshly formed political alliances with changing partners and the maintenance of a European balance of power.

In the last decade—since the bankruptcy of Lehman Brothers catalyzed a global recession—the EU has been dancing with (and around) crises of its own: the eurozone, Brexit, and the revolution (and possible counterrevolution) in Ukraine. But it is my claim that the refugee crisis is the primus inter pares crisis and the dance "partner" that the EU will bring home. The only genuinely pan-European crisis, it puts under question Europe's political, economic, and social model.

The refugee crisis has fundamentally changed the state of play in Europe. It can't be explained solely by the influx of refugees or labor migrants. It is, among many other things, also a migration of arguments, emotions, political identities, and votes. The refugee crisis turned out to be Europe's 9/11.

The Migration Crisis:
Or Why Hasn't History Come to an End?

A little more than a quarter-century ago, in what now seems like the very distant year of 1989—the annus mirabilis that saw Germans rejoicing on the rubble of the Berlin Wall—an intellectual and US State Department official neatly captured the spirit of the time. With the end of the

Cold War, Francis Fukuyama argued, all major ideological conflicts had been resolved. The contest was over, and history had produced a winner: Western-style liberal democracy. Taking a page from Hegel, Fukuyama presented the West's victory in the Cold War as a favorable verdict delivered by history itself. The overthrow of communism was the most marvelous of all revolutions not only because it was liberal and peaceful but also because it was a revolution of the mind. "The state that emerges at the end of history is liberal," Fukuyama insisted, "insofar as it recognizes and protects through a system of law man's universal right to freedom, and democratic insofar as it exists only with the consent of the governed."[2] The Western model was the only (i)deal in town. In the near term, some countries might not succeed at emulating this exemplary model. Yet they would have no alternative to trying.

To understand the current crisis of the EU, we must recognize that the European project today is intellectually rooted in the idea of "the end of history." The European Union is a highly risky wager that humankind will progress and develop in the direction of a more democratic and tolerant society. In an ideological context driven by such liberal nostrums of human improvement, the refugee crisis forces a questioning of everything from top to bottom. What is radical about the migration crisis is not that it asks us to give different answers to those questions pondered in 1989 but that it changes the questions altogether. We are on a substantially changed intellectual footing than a quarter century ago.

In Fukuyama's conceptual framework, the central questions humanity would need to confront were clearcut: How can the West transform the rest of the world, and how can the rest of the world best imitate the West? What specific institutions and policies need to be transferred and copied? What books should be translated and reprinted? How can the old institutions be expanded, and what kind of new institutions should be created?

The dawn of the Internet as a mass phenomenon influenced the West's eagerness to endorse Fukuyama's vision of the future. The end of communism and the birth of the Internet seemed to go together, in that the end of history called for a kind of imitation in the sphere of politics and institutions at the same time that it invited innovation in the field of technology and social life. The very word *revolution* migrated from the world of politics to the world of technology. Nineteen-eighty-nine heralded a world where global competition would increase—but among firms and individuals rather than ideologies and states. Fukuyama imagined a global marketplace where ideas, capital, and goods would flow freely while people stayed home democratizing their societies. The very word *migration* with its attendant images of masses of people crossing national borders, was wholly absent from Fukuyama's story. For him, it was the unfettered travel of ideas that really mattered. In his vision, global ideas would be free to cross borders; as a result, a liberal conception would win over hearts and minds.

It is this vision of the world that is in free fall. Only by contesting its major assumptions can we adequately address the risks of the unraveling of the European project. The questions at the heart of the European Union's existential crisis, and posed by the downward spiraling of the liberal order, are not about what the West did wrong in its efforts to transform the world. The questions are how the last three decades have transformed the West itself and how its ambition to export its values and institutions has resulted in a profound identity crisis in Western societies. That so many Europeans unconditionally accept the flow of immigrants as a sign of democracy's failure is symptomatic of the problems du jour. Only a radical rethinking of the unintended consequences of the end of the Cold War can help explain why angry populists are sweeping elections throughout the Western world and why liberal notions of tolerance, cheaply reduced to a caricatured notion of "political correctness," have come to be seen as the enemy of the people.

Rather than ideas, Fukuyama's engine of progress shaping the future, it is the millions of people legally or illegally arriving in the European Union today who will shape twenty-first-century European history. Migrants, in other words, are history's actors who will define the fate of European liberalism. But the centrality of the migration crisis in European politics compels us not only to reimagine the future but also to reinterpret the past.

At the same time that Francis Fukuyama, amid the enthusiastic applause of Western political elites, professed history's end, another US political scientist, University of California Berkeley's Kenneth Jowitt, was suggesting a very different interpretation of the Cold War's finale. For Jowitt, the Cold War's end was hardly a time of triumph and, instead, signaled the onset of crisis and trauma, the seeding of what he called "the new world disorder."[3] A respected Cold Warrior who had spent his career studying how peripheral communist regimes like Ceausescu's Romania mutate the Soviet model, Jowitt challenged Fukuyama's thesis that Leninism's end was "some sort of historical surgical strike leaving the rest of the world largely unaffected." In Jowitt's view, the end of communism "should be likened to a catastrophic volcanic eruption, one that initially and immediately affects only the surrounding political 'biota' (i.e., other Leninist regimes), but whose effects most likely would have a global impact on the boundaries and identities that for half a century have politically, economically, and militarily defined and ordered the world."[4]

For Fukuyama, the post–Cold War world was still bound by a formal order, where borders between states would endure but no longer provide the power and incentive to provoke war and conflict. He envisioned the spreading of a postmodern idea of the state, one in which values trump interests, a suprastate unsurprisingly embodied in the structure of the European Union. Jowitt, by contrast, had a far bleaker view: He envisioned redrawn borders, reshaped identities, proliferating conflicts, and paralyzing uncertainty. He saw the postcommunist period not as an age of imitation with a handful of dramatic events still left but as a painful and dangerous time rife with dystopian, mutated, and unpredictable regimes. In Fukuyama's imagination, Europe was the model for the coming global liberal order. For Jowitt, on the other hand, the old continent was the epicenter of the new world disorder.

Jowitt did agree with Fukuyama that no universal ideology would appear to challenge liberal democracy, but he was anxious about the notion of postideological politics. While Fukuyama did not see his task as answering "the challenges to liberalism promoted by every crackpot messiah around the world" or the strange illiberal thoughts that "occur to people in Albania or Burkina Faso,"[5] Jowitt disagreed. The Berkeley professor foresaw the return of submerged ethnic, religious, and tribal identities. For him, the end of history would augur an age of resentment. The absence of a powerful universalist ideology to confront liberalism meant not the end of revolutions, per se, but rather a trigger for revolts against the very idea of universality and against the Westernized cosmopolitan elites who defended the idea.

Jowitt predicted that in a world flush with connectivity but marked by economic, political, and cultural disparities, we should be ready for explosions of anger and the emergence of "movements of rage" that would spring from the ashes of weakened nation-states. The post–Cold War order was a kind of singles bar, Jowitt suggested: "It's a bunch of people who don't know each other, who, in the lingo, hook up, go home, have sex, don't see each other again, can't remember each other's names, go back to the bar and meet somebody else. So it's a world that's made up of disconnections."[6] A world, in other words, that is rich in experience but fails to establish stable identities and loyalties.

Unsurprisingly, one possible reaction to the uncertainty brought on by globalization is the return of barricades as the desired borders for people and states. In Jowitt's suggestive metaphor, "a barricade is a Roman Catholic marriage. You get married, you can't get divorced."[7] It is exactly the transition from the disconnected world of the 1990s to the barricaded world emerging today that changes the performative role of democratic regimes. Democracy as a regime-type that favors the emancipation of minorities (gay parades, women's marches, affirmative action policies) is supplanted by a political regime that empowers the prejudices of majorities. And it is the political shock caused by the flow of refugees and migrants that is the driving force of the transformation. A study by London's Demos think tank, long prior to Brexit and Donald Trump's presidential victory, showed that opposition to liberal migration policies is the defining characteristic of those supporters of right-wing populist parties[8]. It was liberalism's failure to address the migration problem, rather than the economic crisis or rising social inequality, that explains the public's turn against it. The inability and unwillingness of liberal elites to discuss migration and contend with its consequences, and the insistence that existing policies are always positive sum (i.e., win-win), are what make liberalism for so many synonymous with hypocrisy. This revolt against the hypocrisy of liberal elites is fundamentally reshaping Europe's political landscape.

In the way that the free flow of ideas helped bury communism (and, with it, the Cold War), the flow of people crossing the borders of the EU and the United States has buried the post–Cold War order. The refugee crisis exposed the futility of the post–Cold War paradigm and especially the incapacity of Cold War institutions and rules to deal with the problems of the contemporary world. The 1951 Refugee Convention is among the most spectacular examples of this failure.

The Convention on Refugees is a multilateral UN treaty that defines who a refugee is and adumbrates the rights of individuals who are granted asylum and the responsibility of nations that grant it. Article 1 of the convention, as amended by the 1967 protocol, defines a refugee as follows: "A person who owing to a well-founded fear of being persecuted for reasons of race, religion, nationality, membership of a particular social group or political opinion, is outside the country of his nationality and is unable or, owing to such fear, is unwilling to avail himself of the protection of that country; or who, not having a nationality and being outside the country of his former habitual residence as a result of such events, is unable or, owing to such fear, is unwilling to return to it."[9]

It is clear that the UN convention was framed with Europe in mind, and especially with World War II's refugees and those fleeing the communist East in the early years of the Cold War. The convention was never designed for huge masses of people outside of the West coming to the West. After all, in 1951, the world was still composed mostly of European empires.

In this context, the current migration crisis in Europe and the failure of the Convention on Refugees to effectively contend with it serve as a turning point in reimagining the present world. What until yesterday was conceptualized as a post–Cold War world now looks increasingly like the second coming of decolonization. But if the first round of decolonization involved colonizers returning home, the second, present-day decolonization phase coincides with the "colonized" migrating to the colonial capital. A half-century ago, the colonized asserted the European promise of self-government as the basis for their liberation; now they claim the protection of human rights in order to defend their right to be welcomed in Europe.

In legal and practical terms, it makes abundant sense to articulate a clear distinction between the refugees and migrants. After all, they are not necessarily the same thing. Migrants are leaving their countries in hope of a better life, whereas refugees are fleeing their countries in the hope of saving their lives. But for the purposes of capturing the radical nature of the challenge that the mass movement of people presents to the perceptions of Europeans—the key focus of my analysis—I will use the terms "migrants," "migration crisis," and "refugee crisis" interchangeably.

Despite the vast difference in political contexts, the current moment has similarities with the popular passions of the 1960s. Anxious majorities fear that foreigners are taking over their countries and threatening their way of life and are convinced that the current crisis is enabled by some conspiracy between cosmopolitan-minded elites and tribal-minded immigrants. These threatened majorities represent not the aspirations of the repressed but the frustrations of the empowered. It is not a populism of "the people" held in thrall by the romantic imagination of nationalists, as was the case a century and more ago, but a populism fueled by the demographic projections about the shrinking role of Europe in the world and the expected mass movements of people to Europe. It is a kind of populism for which history and precedent have poorly prepared us.

In many respects, people who vote today for the Far Right in Europe share the sentiments of French *pied noirs* who were forced to leave Algeria at the time of the War of Independence. Both are radicalized and share a sense of betrayal.

Michel Houellebecq's controversial and heatedly discussed novel *Submission* best captures the Molotov cocktail of nostalgia and fatalism ignited by the new populists and pervading a fear-ridden Europe.[10] Francois, the novel's protagonist, is a fortysomething academic at the Sorbonne who lives alone, dines on microwaved dinners, and has casual sex with his female students. He is friendless (and, for that matter, enemy-less) and has no commitments or interests apart from nineteenth-century French literature. Francois peruses porn on the Internet, patronizes sex workers, and bears witness to how the toxic brew of conformism and political correctness brings Islamists to power in France, transforming Francois's country into an enlightened Saudi Arabia. Norwegian writer Karl Ove Knausgaard has observed about the novel that "as a detached list of facts, it seems apparent we are dealing with loneliness, lovelessness, the meaningless . . . and incapacity to feel emotions or establish closeness to others."[11]

But Francois's loneliness, of course, is only a literary vehicle for Houellebecq. *Submission* is an anatomy of the decline and surrender of secular Europe in the face of rising Islam. It is about a Europe that has no will to resist, no leaders to fight for it, and no place to flee to. Francois's twenty-two-year-old mistress, Myriam, joins her parents and takes off for Israel, but Francois himself has nowhere to go. In the tortured imagination of Europe's threatened majorities, immigration is a form of invasion, with outsiders arriving from all directions, and exit for the natives is not an option. In this sense, far-right voters perceive themselves as much more tragic figures than the French *pied noirs* because they have no place to return to.

The Migration of Arguments and Votes

A decade ago, the Hungarian philosopher and former dissident Gaspar Miklos Tamas observed that the Enlightenment, in which the idea of the European Union is intellectually rooted, demands universal citizenship.[12] But universal citizenship requires one of two things to happen: people either enjoy absolute freedom of movement in search of jobs and higher standards of living or the huge economic and political disparities among countries will need to disappear, allowing people to enjoy their universal rights equally in every place. But neither of these is going to happen soon, if ever. (In 2014, *The Economist* estimated on the basis of IMF data that emerging economies might have to wait for three centuries in order to catch up to living standards in the West.) The world today is populated by many failed or failing states in which nobody wants to live and work; moreover, Europe has neither the capacity nor the willingness to allow open borders.

The migration crisis confronts liberalism with a contradiction that is central to its philosophy. How can our universal rights be reconciled with the fact that we exercise them as citizens of unequally free and prosperous societies? The factor that best explains an individual's lifetime income is neither one's education nor the education of one's parents but one's place of birth. Evidence shows that children born in the poorest nations are five times more likely to die before the age of five. Those who survive their early years will lack, in all likelihood, access to basic subsistence services such as clean water and shelter and are ten times more likely to be malnourished. The odds that they will either witness, or themselves suffer, human rights abuses are also significantly increased. If you seek an economically secure life for your children, the best you can do is to make sure your kids will be born in Germany, Sweden, or Denmark. This is ultimately more important than a fancy university degree, a successful business, or having fewer kids.

As Ayelet Shachar argues in her book *The Birthright Lottery*, membership in a state (with its particular level of wealth, degree of stability, and human rights record) has a significant impact on our identity, security, well-being, and the range of opportunities realistically available.[13] By this reading, the most valuable assets Germans have are their German passports; unsurprisingly then, Germans fear the devaluation of their passports no less than they fear inflation. All assets lose value when they become too prevalent and too widely shared. When seen in this context, full membership in an affluent society becomes a complex form of property inheritance: a valuable entitlement that is transmitted—by law—to a restricted group of recipients under conditions that perpetuate the transfer of this precious entitlement to their heirs. This inheritance carries with it an immensely valuable bundle of rights, benefits, and opportunities. Ninety-seven percent of the global population—more than six billion persons—are assigned lifelong membership by the lottery of their birth and either choose or are forced to keep it that way.

It is this birth-right lottery that challenges the major promise of liberal politics and defines the central role of migration in global affairs. In today's connected world, migration is the new revolution—not the twentieth-century revolution of the masses, but a twenty-first century exit-driven revolution enacted by individuals and families. It is inspired not by ideologically painted pictures of a radiant, imaginary future but by Google Maps photos of life on the other side of the border. Migrants are hardly "the virtual vanguard of the gigantic masses," as fashioned by radical theorists like Alain Badiou but are rather lonely revolutionaries.[14] They don't write (or read) manifestos—communist or otherwise. To succeed, this new revolution doesn't require a coherent ideology, political movement, or even leadership. A simple crossing of the border of the European Union is more attractive than any utopia. For so many of today's *damnes de la terre*, change means changing your country by leaving, not changing your government by staying put.

In 1981, when researchers at the University of Michigan conducted the first world values survey, they were surprised to learn that a nation's happiness was not determined by material well-being.[15] Back then, Nigerians were as content as West Germans. But thirty-five years later, the situation has changed. Everyone now has a TV set, and the spread of the Internet has made it possible for young Africans or Afghans with a click of a mouse to see how Europeans live and how their schools and hospitals function. Globalization has made the world a village, but this village lives in a kind of dictatorship—a dictatorship of global comparisons. People rarely compare their lives with the lives of their neighbors anymore; they compare themselves with the most prosperous inhabitants of the planet. Raymond Aron was right when he observed five decades ago that "with humanity on the way to unification, inequality between peoples takes on the significance that inequality between classes once had."[16]

The Crisis and the Left

In his reflections on the impact of the refugee crisis on Europe, Slovenian philosopher Slavoj Žižek comments on Elisabeth Kübler-Ross's classic study *On Death and Dying*.[17] In her book, Kübler-Ross offers the well-known scheme of the five stages of how we react upon learning that we have a terminal illness:

1. *denial* ("This can't be happening, not to me.")
2. *anger* ("How can this happen to me?")
3. *bargaining* ("Just let me live to see my children graduate.")
4. *depression* ("I'm going to die, so why bother with anything?")
5. *acceptance* ("I can't fight it, I may as well prepare for it.")

For Žižek, the reaction of public opinion and the authorities in western Europe to the flow of refugees from Africa and the Middle East follows a similar combination of disparate reactions. There was denial: "It's not so serious, let's just ignore it." There is anger: "Refugees are a threat to our way of life, with Muslim fundamentalists hiding among them, they should be stopped at any price!" There is bargaining: "OK, let's establish quotas and support refugee camps in their own countries!" There is depression: "We are lost; Europe is turning into Europastan!" What is lacking in his view is acceptance, which, in this case, would have meant a consistent all-European plan for dealing with the refugees.

The contradiction between the universal nature of rights and their actual exercise in a national context is at the heart of the current crisis on the Left in the face of the flow of refugees. Žižek, one of the cultural icons of the Left, inspired a reactionary flood when at the peak of the refugee crisis, he insisted that "the defense of one's own way of life does not exclude ethical universalism" and that in order to preserve its progressive role in society, the Left should retreat from its decades-old war against Eurocentrism. After all, in the 1970s, it was Western leftists who passionately claimed the right of rural communities in India to defend their way of life and to resist globalization. Now it's generally right-wing parties that claim the right of prosperous European communities to defend their way of life and to resist those refugees who aspire to live in Europe as they have lived in their own countries. The Left is struggling with how to respond to this new reality.

The European center-left is also facing its own identity crisis, as it has been gravely weakened electorally in these years of mass migration. Social democratic parties throughout the continent are themselves in free fall as the worker's vote flees to the Far Right. In Austria, almost 90 percent of blue-collar workers voted for the far-right candidate in the second round of the May 2016 presidential elections. In the German regional elections, more than 30 percent of that same group supported the reactionary Alternative for Germany. In the French regional elections in December 2015, the National Front reached 50 percent among working-class voters. And perhaps most surprisingly, those voting most defiantly for "leave" in the UK's Brexit referendum were from traditional "safe" labor seats in the north of England.

It is now clear that the post-Marxist working class, which today believes neither in its vanguard role nor in a global anticapitalist revolution, has no reason to be internationalist. The Left-Right division that was structurally fundamental for the European model of democratic politics has lost its power to represent societal divisions. In the

clarifying words of David Goodhart, the former editor of
Prospect magazine,

> The old divides of class and economic interest have
> not disappeared but are increasingly over-laid by a
> larger and looser one—between the people who see
> the world from Anywhere and the people who see it
> from Somewhere. Anywheres dominate our culture
> and society. They . . . have portable 'achieved' identi-
> ties, based on educational and career success, which
> makes them generally comfortable and confident
> with new places and people. The Somewhere people
> are by definition more rooted and usually have 'as-
> cribed' identities—Scottish farmer, working class Ge-
> ordie, Cornish housewife—based on group belonging
> and particular places, which is why they often find
> rapid change more unsettling.[18]

The conflicts between Anywheres and Somewheres,
between globalists and nativists, and between open societies and closed societies have become more important in shaping voters' political identities than previous
class-based identities. Among the many electoral maps
published after the last US elections, one captures this particularly well, showing that although Trump-land covers
around 85 percent of the land mass of the United States,
those living in Clinton-land make up roughly 54 percent
of the population. If we imagine these regions as two countries, we notice immediately that Clinton-land, composed
of coastal regions and urban islands, suggests nineteenth-
century Britain, while Trump-land more resembles the
landmasses of Eurasia governed by Russia and Germany.

The political struggle between Clinton and Trump was one between sea power and land power, between people who think in terms of space and people who think in terms of place. These new dividing lines help explain the abject failure of traditional social democratic parties to drum up electoral support despite the fact that anticapitalist sentiments have skyrocketed, particularly among the younger generation. The disappearance of an internationally minded working class signals a major realignment in European politics.

No longer is it surprising that the new postutopian populism fails to plot on conventional left-right axes. Unlike the Catholic Church or the communists of old, the new populism lacks any catechetical or pedagogical ambitions. New populist leaders don't fantasize about changing their societies. They don't imagine people in terms of what they might become; they like them just the way they are. Empowering people without any common project is the ambition of the new populism. In this sense, the new populism is perfectly suited to societies where citizens are consumers above all else and view their leaders as waiters who are expected to move quickly in fulfilling their wishes.

Human Rights and the Crisis

The refugee crisis has precipitated the decline of human rights discourse as the dominant discourse in European politics. "People think of history in the long term," Philip Roth writes in *American Pastoral*, "but history, in fact, is a very sudden thing." Nothing illustrates this better than the way we think about human rights. People are tempted to believe that the rights movement is as old as humanity itself. But as Harvard historian and legal scholar Samuel Moyn convincingly argues, the birth date of the human rights movement is relatively recent, sometime in the 1970s. Further, in order to understand properly the popularity of the human rights paradigm, we should recognize that it is a substitute for both nation-centered utopias and other internationalist utopias like socialism.

In fact, it is the postutopian nature of human rights that has made it a natural ideology for the end-of-history, post-1989 world. In the 1990s, world opinion took it as self-evident that the rights of man transcend the country in which one is born. The irresistible attraction of so-called fundamental freedoms was rooted in the fact that they were separated from the capacities of the state. It was commonplace that a lack of state resources could not be used as an excuse for treating citizens unjustly. The insistence of political theorists such as Stephen Holmes that rights have costs, and that divorcing the capacity of the state from the ability of the regime to make rights real, has been ignored.[19] But in the course of the refugee crisis, the debate on refugees and migrants has been transformed from a discussion of rights and economics into a security discourse. Governments and publics alike argue that their moral responsibility can't be divorced from their capacity to help and from the risks that newcomers present to their societies.

The perverse effect of this turn of the argument is that Europeans have started to question what they formerly embraced. Open borders are no longer a sign of freedom but are now a symbol of insecurity. As Kelly Grennhill observed, Europeans have been shocked to learn that since 1951 when the Refugee Convention came into force, there have been at least 75 attempts globally by state and non-state actors to use displaced people as political weapons. Their objectives have been political, military, and economic, ranging from the provision of financial aid to full-scale invasion and assistance in effecting regime change. In nearly three-quarters of these historical cases, the coercers achieved at least some of their articulated objectives. In well over half of the documented cases, they obtained all or nearly all of what they sought, making this rather unconventional instrument of state-level influence more effective than either economic sanctions or traditional, military-backed coercive diplomacy.[20]

What Europeans found particularly scary in a world of mutually assured disruption is the fact that using migrants as instruments of pressure proved to be particularly successful when used against liberal democracies.

If Europeans tended to see the spread of democracy as a precondition for a secure and prosperous world, the migration crisis has now radically challenged this assumption. Support for democracy beyond Europe's borders has cratered—collateral damage, one might say, from the migration crisis. If Europeans had thought that exporting their political system would bring stability in a fragile world, now they were inclined to agree with Russian president Vladimir Putin that the spread of democracy can be a trigger for destabilization. Were it metaphysically feasible, many Europeans might likely vote for Libyan leader Muammar Gadafi to be resurrected and reinstalled in power. In the new European consensus, he might be a dictator, but he is a dictator protecting Europe from unwelcome migrants.

In this way, the migration crisis not only shifted the Left-Right balance in European politics and undermined the liberal consensus governing Europe for decades but also provoked an identity crisis on both the left and the right and upended the very arguments the European Union has used to justify its existence. Europe no longer comports itself as a model of the world to come. The European Union is now advertised, at least by a good number of its supporters, as the last hope for a fortressed continent.

A Revolt against Tolerance

In the 1990s, globalization meant the opening of borders for ideas, goods, and capital and was celebrated as a force for the democratization of the world. That is no longer the case. As early as 1994, Edward Luttwak warned that the spread of global capitalism could spark a return of fascism. "It is not necessary to know how to spell *gemeinschaft* and *gesellschaft* to recognize the Fascist predisposition engendered by today's turbocharged capitalism," he wrote.[21] Many now would countenance his view as prescient. The idea of "creative destruction" was at the very heart of our experience with globalization. But if a decade ago we preferred to focus on the "creative," now the focus is, regrettably, on the "destruction."

Tolerance and civility were long the defining characteristics of the European Union. Today they are often perceived as the EU's core vulnerabilities. A revolt against tolerance is paradoxically popular among both populists and liberals: whereas populists contend that our societies are "browning" by being "polluted" by nonwhite races, cultures, and religions and that Europe is unable or unwilling to defend its values, liberals fear that societies are "browning" but in the sense that a growing number of people share the ideology of the brownshirts of National Socialist Germany.

"Identity, it appears, is like sin," claimed the late Samuel Huntington. "However we may oppose it, we cannot escape it."[22] It is shocking to bear witness to how liberal, tolerant Western societies can descend into the worst kind of identity politics. The fear of a return of the illiberal 1930s is widespread among today's European elites—though it is often discussed in psychological (rather than sociological) terms. In the 1930s and 1940s, those German émigrés fortunate to leave the country were haunted by the question of whether fascism could emerge in their new homelands. They were uncomfortable explaining authoritarianism only in terms of German national character or class politics and were genuinely frightened by the prospect of the global spread of fascist ideologies. They were obsessed with the irrationality of the masses, but some of them were tempted to look at authoritarianism as a stable characteristic of individuals or a certain type of personality. In the 1950s, Theodor Adorno spearheaded the first major study on the "authoritarian personality." Since then, the original hypothesis has been significantly reformulated and refined, and research on the psychological sources of authoritarian politics has gone through many rearticulations. Nonetheless, the appeal of the approach remains strong.

The relevance of the psychological approach to studying political changes in today's Western societies is usefully demonstrated in Karen Stenner's 2005 book *Authoritarian Dynamic*.[23] In it, Stenner demonstrates that the demand for authoritarian rule is not a stable psychological trait. Rather, it is a psychological predisposition of individuals to become intolerant when they perceive increased levels of threat. For Jonathan Haidt, "It's as though some people have a button on their foreheads, and when the button is pushed, they suddenly become intensely focused on defending their in-group, kicking out foreigners and nonconformists, and stamping out dissent within the group."[24] And what pushes this button is not simply any peril but what Stenner calls a "normative threat"—when an individual has the feeling that the integrity of the moral order is endangered, that "we" to which an individual belongs seems to be falling apart, or when she feels threatened by the direction in which history seems to be heading. Experiments have demonstrated that people are far readier to tolerate migrants not only when they judge their number acceptable but also when they see signs of their successful integration.

While psychologists insist that people are always pondering the questions "How many of them are among us?" and "How ready are they to become like us?" answers become dramatically more negative when people start to suspect that the flow of foreigners is out of control. It is fear of a collapsing moral order rather than one's concrete situation that triggers an individual's turn against foreigners and others perceived as threatening. The success of political leaders like Donald Trump can best be explained as the ability to persuade American voters that a certain line has been crossed. Similarly, the victory of the Leave campaign in Britain can be explained by the fact that for several years more than half of Britons have agreed with the following statement: "Britain has changed in recent times beyond recognition, it sometimes feels like a foreign country, and this makes me feel uncomfortable."

In his great play *Rhinoceros*, Eugene Ionesco captures the moment when a society, frightened by the emergence of a rhinoceros, is overnight transformed into a society of rhinoceroses. Ionesco was inclined to conceptualize the crisis of liberalism and the rise of fascism and communism in prewar Europe as a pathological conformism driven by collective madness. Karen Stenner, by contrast, stresses the existence of invisible lines demarking a moral order that when crossed can transform a tolerant citizen of liberal democracy into an angry follower of the extreme right. It is telling that the strongest predictor for who voted in favor of Brexit is one's position on the death penalty. Those who demanded the return of the death penalty were the ones most likely to vote for Brexit.

In this sense, a major impact of the refugee crisis on European politics is the moral panic that it has provoked, a sense that the situation has spiraled out of control. The myriad acts of openness toward refugees fleeing war and persecution that we saw in 2015 in places like Germany or Austria are today overshadowed by their inverse: a raging anxiety that these same foreigners, warmly welcomed a year ago, will compromise Europe's welfare model and historic culture and that they will destroy our liberal societies. Fear of Islamic terrorism and a general anxiety over the unfamiliar are at the core of Europe's moral panic. In January 2017, the polling firm YouGov found that

81 percent of French, 68 percent of Britons, and 60 percent of Germans expected a major terrorist attack to take place in their country over the next year.[25] The prospect of a future in which the European Union's borders are constantly stormed by refugees or migrants erodes the trust Europeans have placed in their political system.

But beyond fears of immigration, technological change is inspiring its own form of anxiety. The fear of a barbarian invasion coexists with a fear of a robot-driven transformation of the workplace. In the technological dystopia that we see dawning, there will be no jobs left for human beings. According to a recent UK government study, over the next thirty years, 43 percent of current jobs in the EU will be automated.

How society will function when work is a privilege and not a right or duty is not a theoretical question. Y Combinator, a big start-up incubator, has already announced it will conduct a basic income experiment with roughly one hundred families in Oakland, California, giving them between $1,000 and $2,000 a month for up to a year, no strings attached, to see what people do when they do not need to work to earn a living. The prospect of a jobless future is a major intellectual and existential challenge. How people will be capable of producing meaning in their lives in a postwork society is a question no less pressing than how democracy itself can function in a posttruth political world.

In the demographic dystopia, citizens face a choice no less stark. In order to ensure their prosperity, Europeans need to open their borders; yet such openness threatens to annihilate their cultural distinctiveness. Alternatively, Europeans could shut their borders, but then they would need to be prepared for a steep decline in the overall standard of living and a future where everyone will need to work until physical debility makes it impossible.

The Migration Divide or a Clash of Solidarities?

The refugee crisis is not only impelling Europeans to become skeptical about their own political model; it is also bitterly dividing the European Union and reanimating an East-West divide that had been bridged after 1989. What we are seeing in Europe today is not what Brussels likes to describe as a *lack of solidarity*, but it's rather a *clash of solidarities*: national, ethnic, and religious solidarities are chafing against our obligations as human beings. And this clash of solidarities plays out not only within societies but also among nation states.

Over the last decade, a simple glance at opinion polls has been enough to reveal the varying degrees of trust in the EU that prevail in the West and the East. western Europeans as a rule trust their national governments more than they trust Brussels—making clear that they have faith in Brussels to the extent that their national governments are capable of influencing the direction of Europe.

In the East, the logic has been different. The majority of people there are more likely to trust Brussels than their national governments. They had pinned their hopes on technocrats in Brussels proving more competent and less corrupt than their national leaders. The migration crisis upended this dynamic. Germans and Swedes are now less convinced that their governments are capable of shaping the EU's common policies, while eastern Europeans, still skeptical about the competence and honesty of their national governments, now place more faith in them than in Brussels. They see them ready to defend what lies squarely in the national interest. In short, migration has brought a renationalization of politics and a concomitant resurrection of the East-West divide, if indeed it ever really disappeared.

The question of whether the divide ever disappeared is raised in a particularly literal way by a recent study showing that Germans overestimate the distance between pairs of cities more when one of the cities was found in the former West Germany and the other from the former East Germany than they do when the two cities were both found in one of the countries. And the extent of overestimation is more pronounced for those who take a dim view of German unification. What this may intimate is that the unification of Europe has always been far more a dream than a reality. And it is the return of the East-West divide, more than any other political development, that fuels fears of a wholesale or even partial disintegration of the EU.

In reality, all the crises that Europe faces today divide the union one way or another. The eurozone crisis divides the union over a north-south axis. Brexit highlights the division between the core and the periphery. The Ukraine crisis divides Europe into hawks and doves with respect to dealing with Russia. But it is the east-west divide that reemerged after the refugee crisis that threatens the future survival of the union itself.

Eastern Europe's Compassion Deficit

"I find it difficult to comprehend," German president Joachim Gauck once confessed, "how nations whose citizens were once politically oppressed and who experienced solidarity can withdraw their solidarity for the oppressed from other places."[26] Why is it that central Europeans have become so estranged from the fundamental values that underpin the European Union and show so little solidarity with the sufferings of others?

The scandal of eastern European behavior as viewed from the West is not in the readiness to build fences to keep out refugees but the claim that "we do not owe anything to these people." Migration is also a divisive issue in the West, with each terrorist attack increasing the share of Germans unhappy with Chancellor Merkel's open borders policy. But while in Germany almost 10 percent of the population took part in various volunteer initiatives aimed at assisting asylum seekers, the public in Eastern Europe (aside from a relatively small number of die-hard liberals) remains largely unmoved by the plight of the refugees. That's why leaders there have lambasted Brussels's decision to redistribute refugees among EU member states. Prime Minister Robert Fico of Slovakia has asserted that his country would be prepared to accept only Christians (since there are no mosques in Slovakia, he argued, Muslims would be lost in his country). The leader of the governing Law and Justice Party in Poland, Jarosław Kaczyński, warned that accepting refugees would be a public health risk because of the allegedly dangerous diseases migrants carry with them. Hungarian prime minister Viktor Orbán contends that the European Union's moral duty is not to help the refugees but to guarantee general security. Keeping consistent with his messaging, on October 2, 2016, Orbán organized a referendum in which more than 98 percent of those voting (44 percent of eligible voters went to the polls, falling short of the 50 percent required to make the referendum valid) expressing opposition to admitting foreigners into the country.

What is striking is that with respect to attitudes toward refugees, Catholic Poland is no different than Orthodox Romania and the economically advantaged Czech Republic no more welcoming than the much poorer Bulgaria.

Central European resentment of refugees looks especially odd if we take into account three realities. First, for most of the twentieth century, people in Central and Eastern Europe were preoccupied either with emigrating or with taking care of immigrants. It is enough to remind ourselves that at the end of the nineteenth century and the beginning of the twentieth, the great preoccupation was the "Polonization of the West," in much the same way that many in Germany today are anxious about Islam. Second, there are actually very few refugees in central and eastern European countries. In 2015, the number of refugees who entered Slovakia amounted to a whopping 169 people, and only 8 of them asked to stay. (A poster by the Two-Tailed Dog Party, a group founded by Hungarian prankster artists, ask readers to ponder the amusing fact that Hungarians are more likely to see UFOs in their lifetime than migrants.)

Third, and with tragic irony, Central European economies urgently need migrants. As a consequence of the post-1989 wave of emigration, eastern European societies suffer from declining populations and therefore face deep problems with sustaining their welfare systems. Since the end of communism, 2.5 million people have moved away from Poland, 3.5 million have exited Romania, and Lithuania's population has fallen from 3.5 million to 2.9 million—with numbers continuing to fall.

Why then are eastern Europeans so hostile to refugees? The case of Bulgaria is especially illuminating. The number of refugees who came to Bulgaria after the tragedy of the Balkan Wars and World War I amounted to a quarter of its population (and with the assistance of the League of Nations, Bulgarians managed to provide food and shelter to all of them). Bulgaria then looked like Jordan and Lebanon today, and Bulgarians are justifiably proud that in a very short time they succeeded at integrating so many people.

Why did Bulgarians reach out then and yet refuse to do the same now? The answer is straightforward: a century ago, the people asking for shelter were ethnic Bulgarians. Now they are not. Bulgarians don't believe that the solidarity they once deemed necessary for their own people should be extended to others fleeing war and persecution. In fact, there are more Bulgarians who volunteer today to administer "civic arrests" of refugees who illegally crossed the border than those who volunteer to help them. The refugee crisis has made it clear that eastern Europe views the very cosmopolitan values on which the European Union is based as a threat, while for many in the West it is precisely those cosmopolitan values that are at the core of the new European identity.

Although eastern European hostility toward refugees may be shocking to many, it should not be surprising. It has its roots in history and demography and the twisted paradoxes of the postcommunist transition, while at the same time representing a Central European version of a popular revolt against globalization.

Chapter 1

History matters in Central and Eastern Europe, and very often the region's historical experience contradicts some of the promises of globalization. More so than any other place in Europe, central Europeans are aware of the advantages but also the darker sides of so-called multiculturalism. Eastern European states and nations emerged late in the nineteenth century, and they did so almost simultaneously. While in western Europe it was the legacy of the colonial empires that shaped encounters with the non-European world, Central European states were born of the disintegration of Europe's continental empires—Germany, Austro-Hungary, Russia—and the processes of ethnic cleansing that followed. The nineteenth-century ethnic mosaic of Western Europe was generally harmonious, like a Caspar David Friedrich landscape, whereas that of Central Europe resembled more an expressionist canvas by Oskar Kokoschka. While in the prewar period Poland was a multiethnic, multiconfessional society in which more than a third of the population was German, Ukrainian, or Jewish, today Poland is one of the most ethnically homogeneous societies in the world with 98 percent of the population ethnically Polish. For many of them, the return to ethnic diversity is a return to the troubled times of the interwar period. After all, it was the destruction and expulsion of Jews and Germans that enabled the formation of national middle classes in central Europe. And while the European Union is founded on the French notion of the nation (where belonging is defined as loyalty to the institutions of the republic) and the German notion of the state (powerful länder and a relatively weak federal center), Central European states were built on the reverse: they combine a French admiration for the centralized and all-powerful state with the idea that citizenship means common descent and shared culture, as held by the Germans. In the view of French political scientist Jacques Rupnik, central Europeans have been particularly outraged by German criticism directed against them during the refugee crisis. It was precisely from nineteenth-century Germans that central Europeans borrowed the idea of the nation as cultural unity.

But central Europe's resentment of contemporary refugees is rooted not only in its long history but also in the experiences of the postcommunist transition. What followed communism and the raft of liberal reforms was a pervasive cynicism. Central Europe may lead the world in the level of mistrust of public institutions. Brecht is no longer part of the school curriculum, but most eastern Europeans would still sign on to his notion that "for this world we live in, none of us is bad enough."[27] Faced with an influx of migrants and haunted by economic insecurity, many eastern Europeans feel betrayed by their hope that joining the European Union would jumpstart prosperity and end their crisis-filled existence. Being more impoverished than western Europeans, they wonder how anyone can expect them to express spontaneous humanitarian solidarity. The reaction of eastern Europeans to globalization is not so different, frankly, than that of Trump's white working-class supporters. They both view themselves as forgotten losers.

Eastern Europeans' hostile reaction to refugees and migrants is also rooted in a sense of betrayal that many feel when they hear European leaders describe mass migration as a win-win proposition. In his book *Exodus*, Oxford economist Paul Collier makes clear that while the migration of people from poor countries to the West is beneficial to the migrants and as a whole benefits host societies, it can negatively affect the lower classes of these same host societies and particularly the chance that their children will have better lives.[28] The resistance of liberals to conceding any negative effects of migration has triggered the antiestablishment (and particularly anti-mainstream-media) reaction that is convulsing political life in democracies in so many places today.

Curiously, demographic panic is one of the least discussed factors shaping eastern Europeans' reaction toward refugees. But it is a critical one. Nations and states have an unfortunate habit of disappearing in the recent history of eastern and central Europe. In the last twenty-five years, around 10 percent of Bulgarians have left the country in order to live and work abroad. According to United Nations projections, Bulgaria's population is expected to shrink by 27 percent by 2050. Alarm over "ethnic disappearance" can be discerned in many of the small nations of Eastern Europe. For them, the arrival of migrants signals their exit from history, and the popular argument that an aging Europe needs migrants only strengthens the growing sense of existential melancholy. When you watch on television scenes of elderly locals protesting the settlement of refugees in their depopulated villages where not a single child has been born for decades, your heart breaks for both sides—the refugees, but also the old, lonely people who have seen their worlds melt away. Is there going to be anyone left to read Bulgarian poetry in one hundred years?

In the politics of threatened majorities, a democratic imagination is a demographic one. The nation, not unlike God, is one of humanity's shields against the idea of mortality. It is in the memory of our family and our nation that we hope to continue living after our death. The lonely individual is mortal in a different way than the person attached to a particular group. It is thus not surprising that the demographic imagination shapes not only society's hostilities to foreigners but also its negative reactions to social changes like gay marriage. Postcommunist societies, most of which are very secular as a rule, are quite tolerant when it comes to sexual life. But for many conservatives, gay marriages signify fewer kids and further demographic decline. For an eastern European nation haunted by low birth rates and migration, the endorsement of gay culture is like endorsing your own disappearance.

The demand of central Europeans that borders be closed is also a belated reaction to the impact of emigration from the region that followed their opening in 1989. In a popular joke, three Bulgarian men dressed in Japanese costumes and armed with swords walk on the streets of Sofia: "Who are you and what do you want?" asks the puzzled crowd. "We are the seven samurais and we want to make this country a better place." "But why are there only three of you then?" they are asked. "Because only three of us stayed; the rest are all abroad." Official statistics tell us that 2.1 million Bulgarians were living outside the country in 2011. The figure is exceptionally high for a country with just slightly more than seven million persons.

The opening of the borders was both the best and the worst thing to happen to Bulgarian society after the fall of the Berlin Wall. "I can only love what I am free to leave," wrote East German dissident Wolf Biermann in the 1970s.[29] For half a century, Bulgarians were asked to love a country they were not free to leave, so opening the borders was understandably a welcome development. An opinion poll twenty-five years after the fall of the Wall showed Bulgarians consider the opening of the borders the greatest achievement of the postcommunist period.

But mass emigration, mostly of people between the ages of twenty-five and fifty, has dramatically hurt Bulgaria's economy and politics. What started in 1989 as a democratic revolution has turned into a demographic counterrevolution. The IMF calculated that if the outflow of people continues at present rates, central Europe, eastern Europe, and southeastern Europe will lose around 9 percent of their expected GDP for the period 2015–30. Businesses in the region constantly complain about the shortage of qualified labor. Eastern European health systems are deprived of well-trained nurses who prefer to earn several times more by taking care of a single family in London than by practicing their profession in a low-paying local hospital. The majority of Bulgaria's best students don't even apply to Bulgarian universities, thus depriving them of talent and ambition. Bulgarians are the second-largest foreign student community in Germany after the Chinese. And although most of the people who leave plan to come back, returning is easier said than done. People who have left the country early in their lives lack local networks and an understanding of local realities. They are often dispirited to find that they are welcomed back with less enthusiasm than they had hoped. Out of sight is out of mind. The very fact that "getting out" is so popular makes returning an unattractive option. There is the perverse sense that only "losers" seek to return home.

If we wonder why Bulgarians have tended to be governed by the wrong people in recent years, we have to ask if mass emigration could be the culprit. The citizen who decides to leave his country hardly has the reform of the country he has left in mind. He is interested in changing his own lot in life, not the lives of others. The mass anti-government protests that took place in Bulgaria in 2013 captured well the paradox of open borders. Protesters on the street were shouting "we do not want to emigrate," but in reality, some of them did because it is easier to go to Germany than to make Bulgaria function like Germany. There are only two effective ways to deal with political and economic stagnation, preaches a popular Bulgarian joke—one is Terminal 1 and the other is Terminal 2 (of Sofia's international airport).

The biggest beneficiaries of the opening of the borders turned out to be the brilliant individual émigrés, the bad eastern European politicians, and the xenophobic western European parties. Twenty-five years later, many eastern Europeans have started to have second thoughts about how much their countries have truly benefited from a regime of openness.

The failed integration of the Roma also contributes to eastern Europe's compassion deficit. Eastern Europeans fear foreigners in part because they mistrust the capacity of their societies and the state to integrate the "others" already in their midst. The story of the Roma is among the most disturbing in contemporary Europe.

In many eastern European countries, the Roma are not simply unemployed but unemployable because they drop out of school very early and fail to acquire the skills needed for the twenty-first-century job market. At the end of 2016, the EU Agency for Fundamental Rights released a report on the Roma situation based on

thousands of face-to-face interviews in the nine countries with sizable Roma populations.[30] All of these are
eastern and southern European states, six of them post-
Communist. Most of Europe's six million Roma people
live in those countries. The survey found that 80 percent
of Roma live below an already low poverty line, a third
have no running water, and one in ten have no electric-
ity. Employment rates for men and women are 34 and
16 percent, respectively, and two-thirds of Roma people
between the ages of sixteen and twenty-four neither work
nor attend school. Roma kids tend to drop out early, and
even if they don't, they are likely to be held back in lower
grades more often than their non-Roma peers. Previous
surveys of European Roma showed similar levels of poverty, unemployment, and poor education. Opinion surveys, including the latest Pew Global report on attitudes
toward minorities in Europe, show that the Roma are
viewed less favorably than Muslims and far less favorably than Jews.[31] Ordinary citizens who live next to the
Roma (which means, in most cases, that they can't afford
to move away) are even more vehement in accusing the
Roma of being unable to and uninterested in integrating.

Experiences of hard-to-assimilate minorities appear
to get conflated. In Bulgaria, according to Gallup, 60 percent believe that Roma integration is impossible, and
the majority is convinced that all integration policies are
doomed to fail. Roma are among us, but they are never
becoming one of us. It is the failure of Roma integration
that makes eastern Europeans assume that their countries
"just cannot do it." And the fact that eastern Europeans
and refugees coming from Asia or the Middle East quite
often end up as competitors on the Western job market

hardly makes eastern Europeans more open to the politics of integrating them. On the contrary, in central Europe, anti-Roma sentiments have contributed to majorities turning against the rhetoric of human rights. If in western Europe the debate around human rights is about "our rights," then in central Europe it is about "their rights." Human rights activists are blamed for ignoring the problems of majorities and inspiring an unhealthy competition for victimhood status.

In the end, however, it is central Europe's deeply rooted mistrust toward a cosmopolitan mind-set that divides East and West. Eastern Europe does not have a colonial history and thus lacks a sense of guilt, but it also lacks a shared fate that often accompanies colonial encounters. The current resentment of cosmopolitanism, which in many aspects reminds us of the successes of the anticosmopolitan campaigns in Stalinist-dominated Europe, is well captured by the growing eagerness of voters to support nativist political leaders whose major advantage is that they are not interested in the world, do not speak foreign languages, have no interest in foreign cultures, and avoid visiting Brussels. Polish foreign minister Witold Waszczykowski speaks for many when he expresses his resentment of EU-style liberalism marked by "a new mixture of cultures and races, a world made up of cyclists and vegetarians, who only use renewable energy and who battle all signs of religion." In his view, "What moves most Poles is tradition, historical awareness, love of country, faith in God, and normal family life between men and women."[32] In the first post–Cold War decade, Europe, and particularly the European Union, was the model liberalism embraced. Being a normal country was the dream of eastern European society. The West's normality was embodied by its prosperity, civility, and economic success. Three decades later, postmodern Europe is viewed by many eastern Europeans as culturally abnormal.

The attitudinal divide between Europe's West and East on the issues of diversity and migration strongly resembles the divide between the large cosmopolitan capital cities and the countryside within Western societies themselves. They are two worlds deeply mistrustful of each other. It is interesting to note that while the generational differences are very sharp when it comes to, say, tolerance of sexual minorities, and while young eastern Europeans are much more liberal than their parents, when the discussion turns to migration, the generation gap ends: the young are as hostile as the older generations.

The Austrian-Jewish writer Joseph Roth spent most of the interwar years wandering around Europe and taking refuge in the lobbies of grand hotels. For Roth, such hotels were the last remnants of the old Habsburg Empire, a postcard from a lost world, a place where he felt at home. Some Central European intellectuals do share Roth's nostalgia for the cosmopolitan spirit of the empire, but ordinary citizens of central Europe do not. They feel comfortable in their ethnic states and mistrust those whose hearts lie in Paris or London, whose money is in New York or Cyprus, and whose loyalty is to Brussels. In the words of historian Tony Judt, "From the outset eastern and 'central' Europeans, whose identity consisted largely in a series of negatives—not Russian, not Orthodox, not Turkish, not German, not Hungarian, and so forth—had provinciality forced upon them as an act of state making. Their elites were obliged to choose between cosmopolitan allegiance to an extraterritorial unit or idea—the Church, an empire, Communism, or, most recently 'Europe'—or else the constricting horizon of nationalism and local interest."[33] Being cosmopolitan and at the same time a "good Pole," "good Czech," or "good Bulgarian" is not in the cards. It is instructive that while Pope Francis was taking in Syrian refugees to live in his house, Catholic Bishops in Hungary and Poland were expressing the same antirefugee sentiments as their governments.

It is this historically rooted suspicion of anything cosmopolitan, and the direct connection between communism and internationalism, that partially explains central Europe's sensitivities when it comes to the refugee crisis.

In making sense of the East-West divide as it concerns the endorsement of cosmopolitan values, we should also bear in mind that in this respect the legacies of Nazism and Communism differ significantly. The German drive for cosmopolitanism was also a way to escape the xenophobic legacy of Nazism, while it could be argued that central Europe's anticosmopolitanism is partially rooted in an aversion to a communist-imposed internationalism. This strange legacy explains why the revolt against cosmopolitan elites takes the form of criticism not only of Brussels but also of anticommunist sentiment, particularly in a moment when majorities have moved to the left in their economic and political views. (In western Europe, 1968 symbolizes the endorsement of cosmopolitan values, while in the east it stands for the re-birth of national sentiments.)

In many aspects, the attitudes of the populist governments in Central and Eastern Europe resemble the behavior and attitudes held by the second generation of migrants in Europe toward their host countries. In the first generation of Central European leaders, politicians like Vaclav Havel made integration into the EU their life's cause and tried to prove that central Europeans could be more European than the Westerners. But the new generation of leaders experiences the constant pressure to adopt European norms and institutions as a humiliation and build their legitimacy around the idea of a national identity in opposition to Brussels.

The paradox of the East-West divide provoked by the refugee crisis is that we are witnessing a convergence of attitudes wherein Germans who were once friendly to refugees start to resemble xenophobic Hungarians. Moreover, the fact that many Germans personally welcomed refugees a year ago makes it morally easier for them to turn against the presence of the foreigners in their countries today. But the convergence of attitudes does not bring any more cohesion to the continent. The paradox of the divisive convergence is that the renationalization of politics makes eastern Europeans feel more like foreigners in western Europe than ever before. In the wake of Brexit, the attacks on eastern Europeans skyrocketed in the UK. Rising hostility to other Europeans can now be detected all over the continent, as a restaurant owner I know in Vienna recently learned. Of Serbian origin, he was quite hostile to refugees from the Middle East and enjoyed lampooning Austrians for their naiveté in welcoming them. But when Austrian attitudes changed, he was stunned to realize that many locals stopped visiting his restaurant on account of the fact that they had heard him speaking Serbian.

The refugee crisis is critical for gauging the prospects of the European Union's chances of survival because it simultaneously reinforces a sense of national solidarity and erodes the chances for constitutional patriotism in the union as a whole. The crisis is thus a turning point in the political dynamics of the European project. It signals a moment when the demand for democracy in Europe has been transformed into a call to defend one's own political community and thus a demand for exclusion rather than inclusion. It also creates a dynamic in which the European project is seen no longer as an expression of liberal universalism but as a sour expression of its defensive parochialism.

Chapter 2

They the People

"Had I been cryogenically frozen in January 2005," writes British historian Timothy Garton Ash, one of Europe's most prominent public intellectuals,

> I would have gone to my provisional rest as a happy European. With the enlargement of the European Union . . . the 1989 "return to Europe" dream of my Central European friends was coming true. EU member states had agreed on a constitutional treaty, loosely referred to as the European constitution . . . It was amazing to travel without hindrance from one end of the continent to another, with no border controls inside the expanding zone of states adhering to the Schengen Agreement and with a single currency in your pocket for use throughout the eurozone.
>
> Madrid, Warsaw, Athens, Lisbon, and Dublin felt as if they were bathed in sunlight from windows newly opened in ancient dark palaces. The periphery of

Europe was apparently converging with the continent's historic core around Germany, the Benelux countries, France, and northern Italy. Young Spaniards, Greeks, Poles, and Portuguese spoke optimistically about the new chances offered them by "Europe." Even notoriously Euroskeptical Britain was embracing its European future under Prime Minister Tony Blair. And then there was the avowedly pro-European Orange Revolution in Ukraine. . . .

Cryogenically reanimated in January 2017, I would immediately have died again from shock. For now there is crisis and disintegration wherever I look: the Eurozone is chronically dysfunctional, sunlit Athens is plunged into misery, young Spaniards with doctorates are reduced to serving as waiters in London or Berlin, the children of Portuguese friends seek work in Brazil and Angola, and the periphery of Europe is diverging from its core. There is no European constitution, since that was rejected in referendums in France and the Netherlands later in 2005 . . . And Brexit brings with it the prospect of being stripped of my European citizenship on the thirtieth anniversary of 1989.[1]

This is how pro-EU Europeans feel today.

In twentieth-century Europe, nondemocratic empires disintegrated under democratic pressure brought to bear by their own subjects. Democrats were the ones who destroyed empires; liberals sought to save and reform them. In 1848, liberals and nationalists were allies within the Habsburg Empire, united by their shared opposition to the authoritarian (but not ethnically specific) center. By 1918, they had become each other's sworn enemies. In

1848, both democrats (most of whom were nationalists as well) and liberals insisted that the people should decide. In 1918, liberals were nervous about the prospect of popular democracy while democrats loathed the idea of being governed by unelected liberal elites. The clash between cosmopolitan liberals and national-minded democrats ended with victory for the nationalists and the death of the Austro-Hungarian Empire.

The European Union, unlike the Habsburg Monarchy, is a "democratic empire," a voluntary quasi-federation of democratic states in which citizens' rights and freedoms are guaranteed and that only democracies may join. Despite this difference, the democracy question is once again at the heart of Europe's troubles. If in the Habsburg case the masses were enchanted with democracy, in today's EU they are stricken with disillusionment. The general mood in Europe these days can be summed up as follows: "One of the reasons many people are skeptical about democracy is because they're right to be." The 2012 "Future of Europe" survey indicated that only a third of Europeans believe their vote counts at the EU level, and a paltry 18 percent of Italians and 15 percent of Greeks believe that their votes count *even in their own country.*[2]

According to a recent survey, the paradoxical effect of the global spread of democracy in the last fifty years is that citizens, in a number of supposedly consolidated democracies in North America and western Europe, have grown more critical of their political leaders.[3] But that's not all. They have also become more cynical about the value of democracy as a political system, less hopeful that anything they do might influence public policy, and more willing to express support for authoritarian alternatives.

The study also shows that "younger generations are less committed to the importance of democracy" and that they are "less likely to be politically engaged."[4]

From today's uncompromising vantage point, a political union capable of backing the euro with a common fiscal policy cannot be accomplished as long as EU member states remain fully democratic. Their citizens will just not support it. Yet the breakup of the common currency could possibly lead to the fragmentation of the union, with one of the end results being a likely rise of authoritarianism on the EU's periphery. Unlike in any earlier period, the objectives of an "ever closer union" and "deeper democracy" are at odds with one another.

The Specter of Populism

In June 2006, when the Slovak Robert Fico won a plurality of the vote and formed a government in coalition with Jan Slota's extreme nationalistic Slovak National Party, the Slovak constitutional court announced that one of its citizens had asked the court to annul the election. The claimant insisted that the republic had failed to create a "normal" system of elections and had therefore violated a citizen's constitutional right to be governed wisely. In the eyes of the claimant, an electoral system that could lead to a motley coalition such as the new Slovak government could not be "normal."

The lone Slovak appellant had a point. The right to be governed wisely can contradict a citizen's right to vote. This is what has always made liberals anxious about democracy. Indeed, those familiar with the work of the influential nineteenth-century French liberal historian Francois

Guizot might suspect that he had been reincarnated in the figure of the Slovak citizen who demanded answers from the constitutional court. That democratic governance can be destructive to the European project is a common concern for many European liberals. For them, George Orwell may have said it best: "Public opinion is no more innately wise than humans are innately kind."[5]

The clearest manifestation of the current fear can be seen in the reaction of European leaders to the greatest victim of the financial crisis: Greece. Unsustainably underwriting a noncompetitive economy while keeping social spending high and suffering from stunning corruption, Greece was the victim of a perfect storm. A hurricane really. In the precrisis decade, EU wages per employee had increased by 30 percent, but in Greece they skyrocketed 85 percent. For public sector wages, it was even worse: a 40 percent increase in the EU, but an astounding 117 percent spike in Greece. By the summer of 2011, it was clear that the EU was the only hope for Greece to avoid bankruptcy and to remain in the eurozone. But external support would come at the price of a costly—in both political and human terms—austerity program. On October 31, 2011, Greek prime minister George Papandreou announced a referendum on a bailout plan proposed by the European Union, the European Central Bank, and the International Monetary Fund (IMF). He asked his countrymen to support the reform measures demanded by the creditors. This was the price of staying in the eurozone.

But the referendum never happened. Three days after announcing it, and following a harsh reaction by Berlin and Brussels, the Greek government shelved the idea and the reforms were voted on in the Parliament instead. It was a painfully clear example of "democracy frustrated." Western European leaders were convinced that Greek citizens should not be permitted a say when the outcome of the vote would affect the fate of a currency belonging to everyone living in the eurozone. Put more harshly, many thought it absurd to suggest that debtors be given a vote on terms they would be offered by creditors. Unsurprisingly, Papandreou's Socialists not only lost the next elections but faded fast as a force in Greek politics more generally. The division of EU member states into a creditors-debtors axis became one of the most devastating outcomes of the euro crisis.

Several years later, a second appearance of the referendum idea emerged on the initiative of Alexis Tsipras and his radical left-wing Syriza Party. This time, we might call it "democracy castrated." The Greeks actually held a vote on July 5, 2015—with the vast majority rejecting (as Tsipras's government had hoped they would) the terms for a new, third bailout by the so-called troika of the IMF, the European Central Bank, and the European Commission. But this heroic resistance to creditors lasted no more than a week. By the next Monday, Tsipras had swallowed a much harsher version of the bailout, agreeing to implement policies that he had only recently deemed "criminal."

The temporary resolution of the Greek crisis was instructive on one fundamental point. For the common European currency to survive, voters of debtor nations must be deprived of their right to change economic policy despite retaining a capacity to change governments. It was the most powerful restatement that the governing formula of the EU—namely, policies without politics in Brussels and politics without policies on the national level—had been reinforced by the crisis. Given what had occurred, it became clear that what Tsipras and Yanis Varoufakis (his finance minister until July 2016) were fighting was less the policies proposed by creditors than being held responsible for acceding to them. The Greek welfare state was transformed into a warfare state. The government was unable to redistribute wealth, so it worked overtime to redistribute blame.

In handling the rebellion from Athens, European leaders faced a stark choice. They could either allow Greece to default and thus put the common currency at risk, destroy the Greek economy, and send the message that in a political union of creditors and debtors there is no place for solidarity—or save Greece on Tsipras's terms and thereby signal that political blackmail works, inspiring populist parties across the continent.

Faced with the dilemma, European leaders identified a third option: to save Greece on such draconian terms that no other populist government would ever be tempted to follow its example. Tsipras is now the living demonstration that there is no alternative to the economic policies of the European Union.

The immediate impact of the agreement was expected: the markets calmed, the Greeks felt demoralized, and the Germans remained skeptical. But did the victory of economic reason over the will of the voters contribute to the survival of the union? That story is far less clear cut.

For many, "democracy" in the EU quickly became code for the political impotence of citizens. Rather than Brussels symbolizing the glory of a common European home, the EU's capital came to represent the unrestricted power of the markets and the destructive power of globalization.

Greeks may have despaired of their failure to resist the imprecations of the market, but their southern European neighbors, the Italians, were primed to celebrate them. Silvio Berlusconi's last act as Italian prime minister in the fall of 2011 was to drive a car through a crowd of protesters who had been taunting him with epithets like "buffoon" and "shame."

As the seventy-five-year-old oligarch and media mogul met with the Italian president to tender his resignation, the streets outside the presidential palace pulsated with chanting demonstrators waving Italian flags and uncorking champagne bottles. In one corner, a choir sang Leonard Cohen's "Hallelujah" accompanied by an impromptu orchestra. Across the way, celebrants formed a conga line. Cars honked their horns and pedestrians broke into song. It had the ambience of a revolutionary moment.

But it was far from it. The fall of Berlusconi was hardly a classic triumph of "people's power." Rather, it was an unequivocal triumph of the power of financial markets. The will of the voters never booted Berlusconi's corrupt and ineffective clique out of office; it was brought about by the explicit joining of financial markets with the commanding bureaucratic heights in Brussels and the European Central Bank's leadership in Frankfurt, all of which imparted the fateful message, "Berlusconi must go." It was also they who picked the former European commissioner Mario Monti, a "technocrat" (and thus not "political"), to be Berlusconi's successor. People on the streets of Rome had every reason to feel ecstatic yet powerless. Berlusconi may be gone, but the voter ceased being the most powerful figure in crisis-torn Italy. The public's celebration of the end of the Berlusconi regime resembled the enthusiasm of Italians upon greeting Napoleon's victorious army in 1796. People on the street were not the agents but the spectators of history.

In Greece's case, Brussels became the symbol of the arrogant elite that shifts the cost of the crisis onto a weak and defenseless Greek people. For Italy, at least for a time, Brussels was the citizens' sole hope to oust an unpopular prime minister and break the oligarchical regime he created. At the heart of the European Union's loss of legitimacy is the fact that, with the deepening of the EU's crisis, Brussels's role as an ally of the people against corrupt national elites dimmed. Italians shifted their hopes for a better life toward populist Euroskeptical parties like Beppe Grillo's Five Star Movement. In a similar way that Italian nationalism inspired by the French Revolution turned against Napoleon, those Italians who celebrated the ousting of Berlusconi's government are today casting their vote for anti-EU parties.

In his book *The Globalization Paradox*, Harvard political economist Dani Rodrik suggests that we have three options to manage tensions between national democracies and globalization.[6] We can restrict democracy in order to gain competitiveness in international markets. We can limit globalization in the hope of building democratic legitimacy at home. Or we can globalize democracy at the cost of national sovereignty. What we cannot have, Rodrik makes clear, is hyperglobalization, democracy, and self-determination simultaneously. But this is precisely what most governments want. They want people to have the right to vote yet are unready for those votes to sanction populist policies. They want to be able to reduce labor costs and ignore social protests while also refusing to enter the murky waters of publicly endorsing an authoritarian strong hand. They favor free trade and interdependence, but they want to be sure that when necessary (in a moment of crisis like the present) they can return to national control of the economy. Instead of choosing between a sovereign democracy, a globalized democracy, or a globalization-friendly authoritarianism, political elites try to redefine democracy and sovereignty in order to make possible the impossible. The outcome is unworkable: you end up with democracy without choices, sovereignty without meaning, and globalization without legitimacy.

What was until recently a competition between two distinctive forms of government—democracy and authoritarianism—has evolved in the wake of the global financial crisis into a competition between two different forms of the statement: "There is no alternative politics." In democratic Europe, the fact that "there is no policy alternative" to austerity has become the mantra of the day: voters can change governments, to be sure, but they are disempowered to change economic policies. By constitutionalizing many macroeconomic decisions (e.g., budget deficits, levels of public debt), Brussels has de facto extricated them from the domain of electoral politics.

In Russia and China, the "no alternative" discourse means that it is impossible to remove their current leaders. The governing elite can be more flexible in experimenting with different economic policies, but what is excluded in Russia and China is the possibility to challenge those in power. People are not allowed to elect "wrong" leaders—therefore, elections are either controlled, rigged, or banned for the sake of "good governance."

In order to assess the role of democracy in the current European crisis, we need to accept that what is driving public sentiment is not a democratic aspiration but a democratic confusion. This leaves the analyst of Europe's political crisis in a trap. At one level, what was true about monarchy more than a century ago (Walter Bagehot's notion that "it is an intelligible government [because] the mass of mankind understand it, and they hardly anywhere in the world understand any other"[7]) is now true of democracy. But there is a growing fear that democracy simply does not work.

To gauge how dissatisfaction with democracy (which often takes the form of a demand for a different democracy) will affect the chances of the European Union's survival, we must make sense of three paradoxes. First, why are Central European voters, who opinion polls tell us constitute some of the continent's most pro-European electorates, ready to put in power anti-EU parties that openly loathe independent institutions such as courts, central banks, and the media? I will call it the "Central European paradox." Second, why has the political mobilization of the younger generations in western Europe, who according to opinion polls are much more liberal and friendly to the union than older voters, not led to the emergence of pan-European pro-EU populist movement? I will call it "West European paradox." And third, why are Europeans so resentful to Brussels's elites when they are the most meritocratic elites in Europe? I will call it "Brussels paradox."

The Central European Paradox

In the last decade, European integration has been widely understood and accepted as the major factor guaranteeing the irreversibility of the democratic changes in the postcommunist countries of central Europe. Much as Europe's welfare state guaranteed a safety net to the most vulnerable members of society, there has been a belief that the European Union is its own safety net for the new democracies from the East. The EU developed institutional mechanisms of peer pressure and carrot-and-stick policies that have the capacity to prevent the backsliding of democratization in its new members. This grand expectation, however, has turned out to be wrong. The electoral victory of Viktor Orbán in Hungary and Jarosław Kaczyński in Poland and the "illiberal turn" in most of central Europe has forced many commentators to upend their view of the "Brussels effect" on the process of democratic consolidation in central Europe.

In the view of political scientists James Dawson and Sean Hanley, marrying the process of democratization to the process of European integration has contributed to the emergence of fair-weather democracies in the East with political elites that lack genuine commitments to liberal values.[8] Even more important is the effect of the European Union serving as a kind of safety net, which mitigates against risk-taking (keeping countries from advancing irresponsible policies) but incentivizes voters to support irresponsible political parties and leaders as a way of signaling disappointment and anger. Why should Poles fear someone like Kaczyński if they know that Brussels will tame him if he goes too far? Paradoxically, the twinning of Europeanization and democratization has turned central Europe into a poster child of democratic illiberalism. In the prophetic words of Hungarian prime minister Viktor Orbán, "A democracy is not necessarily liberal. Just because something is not liberal, it still can be a democracy." Moreover, "One could—and indeed should—say," he insisted, "that societies founded upon liberal principles of organizing a state will likely not be able to sustain their global competitiveness in coming years—rather, it is more likely that they will suffer a setback, unless they manage to reform themselves substantially."[9] In this context, central Europe's slide into illiberalism was not an unintended consequence. It was a choice. And in order to understand this choice, it is important to ascertain what made central Europeans so nervous about liberal democracy in the first place.

The "populist turn" varies in different countries, but we can nonetheless identify commonalities. The rise of populist sentiments signals a return to political polarization and a more confrontational style of politics. It is also a return to more personalized politics in which political leaders play an outsized role and institutions are frequently mistrusted. The Left-Right divide is being replaced by a conflict between internationalists and nativists, and the explosion of fears that it unleashes marks a violent distancing between democracy and liberalism. But populism's key feature is a hostility not to elitism but to pluralism. As Jan Werner-Müller writes in *What Is Populism?*, "Populists claim that they and they alone, represent the people. . . . The claim to exclusive representation is not an empirical one; it is always distinctly moral."[10] Populists do not claim to stand for all Poles, French, or Hungarians, but they insist that they stand for all "true Poles," "true French," and "true Hungarians." The electoral success of the populist parties transforms democracy from an instrument for inclusion into an instrument of exclusion.

The new populist majorities perceive elections not as an opportunity to choose between policy options but as a revolt against privileged minorities—in the case of Europe, elites and a key collective "other," the migrants. In the rhetoric of populist parties, elites and migrants are twins who thrive off of one another: neither is like "us," both steal and rob from the honest majority, neither pays the taxes that it should pay, and both are indifferent or hostile to local traditions.

Despite the deep public mistrust of politicians, it is perplexing why people are nonetheless ready to elect parties eager to dismantle any constraints on government power. This is the conundrum that will help us unpack the Central European paradox.

The decision of the populist governments in Hungary and Poland to take control over their respective constitutional courts, to curb the independence of central banks, and to declare war on independent media and civil society organizations should be alarming for those who are mistrustful of their politicians. But contrary to expectations, the vast majority of Hungarians and a sizable number of Poles were not concerned by their governments' decisions to concentrate power in the hands of each country's executive. How did the separation of powers lose its appeal? Is it because people couldn't distinguish their support for free media or independent courts from the media outlets they blame for disregarding the truth or from the judges they see as corrupt and inefficient? Is it possible that in the eyes of the public the separation of powers is less a way to keep officeholders accountable than another trick up the sleeves of the elites?

The real appeal of liberal democracy is that it defends not only property rights and the right of the political majority to govern but also the rights of minorities, ensuring that those defeated in elections can return to compete in the next contest and don't have to flee, go into exile, or hide underground while their possessions are seized by the victors. The little-remarked downside of this arrangement is that for winners liberal democracy gives no chance for a full and final victory. In predemocratic times—in other words, for the vast bulk of human history—disputes were not settled by peaceful debates and orderly handovers of power. Instead, force ruled. Victorious invaders or the winning parties in a civil war had their vanquished foes at their mercy, free to do with them as they liked. Under liberal democracy, the "conqueror" gets no such satisfaction. The paradox of liberal democracy is that citizens are freer, but they feel powerless. Demand for real victory is a key element in the appeal of the populist parties. "Our country is in serious trouble," was the refrain Donald Trump repeated at his electoral rallies. "We don't have victories anymore. We used to have victories, but we don't have them. When was the last time anyone saw us beating, let's say, China in a trade deal?"[11]

The appeal of populist parties is that they promise an unambiguous victory. They attract those who view the separation of powers (the institution perhaps most beloved by liberals) not as a way to keep those in power accountable but as way for elites to evade their electoral promises. What characterizes populists in power are their constant attempts to dismantle the system of checks and balances and to bring independent institutions like courts, central banks, media outlets, and civil society organizations under their control.

Populist and radical parties aren't just parties; they are constitutional movements. They promise voters what liberal democracy cannot: a sense of victory where majorities—not just political majorities, but ethnic and religious ones too—can do what they please.

The rise of these parties is symptomatic of the explosion of threatened majorities as a force in European politics. They blame the loss of control over their lives, real or imagined, on a conspiracy between cosmopolitan-minded elites and tribal-minded immigrants. They blame liberal ideas and institutions for weakening the national will and eroding national unity. They tend to see compromise as corruption and zealousness as conviction.

What makes anxious majorities most indignant is that while they believe that they are entitled to govern (they are the many after all), they never can have the final say. And so they are ready to blame the separation of powers and other inconvenient principles of liberal democracy for their frustration—and readily endorse parties like Law and Justice in Poland or Fidesz in Hungary that run against those principles.

But populists revolt not only against the institutions of liberal democracy but also against the understanding of politics as a rational calculation of interests. The explosion of conspiracy theories and the growing mistrust toward mainstream media with their claim to be "fair and balanced" is one of the defining characteristics of the populist moment in central Europe. Many analysts prefer to explain the phenomenon in terms of radical changes in communication technologies and blame social media for the prevailing culture of distrust. But the "Facebook effect" can't explain everything.

In 2007, the year the first Law and Justice government headed by Jarosław Kaczyński lost power, the legendary

Polish movie director Andrzej Wajda released his epic film *Katyn*. Over the course of two hours, *Katyn* tells the story of the thousands of Polish prisoners of war—mainly military officers and professional-class civilians—who were murdered in 1940 in the Katyn forest on Stalin's orders. It is actually a film about two crimes: the execution of Polish patriots in the woods near Smolensk and the subsequent cover-up of the truth.

The official version of the tragedy, propagated by the Communist government in postwar Poland, was that the Nazis had been responsible for the executions. But there were Poles who were never ready to live with that lie. One of the main characters in the movie, Agnieszka, seeks to erect a marble headstone for her murdered brother simply bearing the true date of his death—1940—as proof that only the Soviets, who controlled the area at the time, could have carried out the killings. She is persecuted for spreading a conspiracy theory, but she knows she is spreading the truth.

When Kaczyński—back in charge as leader of the once-again-governing Law and Justice Party—announced in a speech in December 2015 that he planned to erect a plaque at the presidential palace in Warsaw as a memorial to his twin brother, he likely saw himself as carrying on the legacy of people like Agnieszka who refused to swallow the Communist lie. Kaczyński's brother, President Lech Kaczyński, perished in 2010 along with ninety-five other members of the Polish elite when his plane crashed upon landing at the Smolensk military airport in western Russia. (In a bizarre twist of history, they were traveling to attend the commemoration of the seventieth anniversary of Katyn.) Jarosław Kaczyński has devoted an inordinate amount of time and energy since the crash working to prove that it was not an accident but a crime perpetrated by the Russians and that the then governing Civic Platform Party, for political or geopolitical reasons, covered up the truth.

The parallels between the two proposed memorials—Agnieszka's and Kaczyński's—are evident. But the analogy is less straightforward. The opening of the Soviet archives in the 1990s left little doubt that in 1940 the Soviets murdered some twenty-two thousand Poles (the precise number of victims is still debated). However, the events of April 10, 2010, when the Polish plane went down in Smolensk, are harder to reconstruct. That said, there is fundamentally no credible evidence to support the Law and Justice Party's suspicions that the crash was an assassination organized by Russians or that Russian air controllers can be held responsible for the catastrophe. In Wajda's film, Agnieszka seeks to build a monument to truth. What Kaczyński is proposing is something quite different: a tribute to a conspiracy theory.

Kaczyński's fight for the truth about Smolensk and the glorification of his brother's legacy have been at the center of the Law and Justice Party's political strategy for the past five years. Kaczyński often personally attended the marches that took place in Warsaw on the tenth of each month to commemorate the crash victims, using them as a tool to help mobilize support for the party. For their part, Poles have seemed increasingly open to persuasion. If, five years ago, most Poles rejected Kaczyński's version of events, and even approved of Russia's handling of the tragedy, today one in three blames Moscow. According to a 2016 opinion poll, belief in the Smolensk cover-up was the strongest predictor of whether or not a person supports Kaczyński.

Poles are not unique in believing, en masse, in the existence of a government cover-up despite a dearth of evidence. According to opinion polls, between half and three-quarters of individuals in various Middle Eastern countries doubt that the planes hijacked on September 11, 2001, were piloted by Arabs; four out of ten Russians think that Americans faked the moon landings; and half of Americans think their government is probably hiding the truth about who was behind the September 11 attacks.[12] For as long as there have been suspicious deaths and powerful people, conspiracy theories and conspiracy theorists have thrived. Scholars tend to agree that such theories are most popular during periods of major social change and that they represent a desire for order in a complex and confusing world. The dozens of reports[13] that "prove" Smolensk was not an accident are classics of the form: carefully footnoted, like a doctoral thesis, and built around both breathtaking generalizations ("when the head of state dies in [an] airplane crash, invariably . . . sabotage is involved")[14] and minute details (the ten thousand small pieces of debris[15] found at the crash site, for instance, which are pointed to as evidence of an explosion).

But what is happening in Poland today has revealed something more: how, in some cases, a shared belief in a particular conspiracy theory can play a role previously reserved for religion, ethnicity, or a well-articulated ideology. It can be a marker of political identity. This helps explain why the Smolensk conspiracy has become a quasi-ideology within the Law and Justice Party. The "assassination hypothesis" helped consolidate a certain "we": we who do not trust the government's lies, we who know how the world really works, we who blame liberal elites for betraying the promise of 1989 revolution. The Smolensk conspiracy was critical for bringing Kaczyński back to power, both because it mined a vein of deep distrust that Polish people feel for any official version of events and because it fit with their self-image as victims of history. But the rise of conspiracy theories highlights another major vulnerability of EU-designed democratic politics—its failure to build political identities.

A decade ago, the British polling agency YouGov undertook a comparative study between a group of political junkies and a similar cohort of young people who actively participated in the *Big Brother* reality show.[16] The distressing finding of the study was that British citizens felt better represented in the *Big Brother* house. It was easier for them to identify themselves with the characters and ideas being discussed. They found it more open, transparent, and representative of people like them. Reality show formats made them feel empowered in the way that democratic elections are supposed to make them feel but don't. Political identities proposed by populist parties are not really that much different from the identities constructed by reality shows. Both are primarily about affirming a similar experience of the world rather than representation of interests.

The populist recoil from the European Union is thus tantamount to a reassertion of more parochial but culturally deeper identities within individual European countries. This movement is driving European politics toward less inclusive, and possibly less liberal, definitions of political community. The sharp Left-Right divide, which has structured European politics since the French Revolution, is gradually blurring. With the rise of a right-wing populism of the sort unknown since the 1920s and 1930s, working classes are now liable to be captured by decidedly antiliberal leaderships. Threatened *majorities*—those who have everything and who therefore fear everything—have emerged as the major force in European politics. The emerging illiberal political consensus is not limited to right-wing radicalism; it encompasses the transformation of the European mainstream itself. It is not what extremists say that threatens Europe; the real threat is what the mainstream leaders no longer say—principally, that diversity is good for Europe.

Threatened majorities today express a genuine fear that they are becoming the losers of globalization. Globalization may have contributed to the rise of numerous middle classes outside the developed world, but it is eroding the economic and political foundations of the middle-class societies of post–World War II Europe. In this sense, the new populism represents not the losers of today but the prospective losers of tomorrow.

The rise of illiberalism in EU-friendly central Europe should help us understand that the existence of pro-EU majorities in most EU member states is not a fail-safe bulwark against the union's breakup. Moreover, what makes the rise of the populist parties dangerous for the survival of the European project is not so much their Euroskepticism—some of them are in fact hardly skeptical—but their revolt against the principles and institutions of constitutional liberalism that serve as the foundations on which the European Union is built.

Chapter 2

The West European Paradox

If you click on "european-republic.eu," you'll catch a glimpse of what the new cosmopolitan revolution from below might look like. The revolutionaries believe that people want Europe, but not the EU as it exists today. In their view, home has little to do with the nationality printed on someone's passport and everything to do with where a person currently lives. The nation itself is therefore the central obstacle to a truly united Europe.

The European Republic website was launched by the charismatic German political scientist Ulrike Guerot and is one of the myriad attempts to create a political platform that is simultaneously anti-status-quo and pro-EU. It is not a new version of the old federalist dream but an attempt to imagine the European Union as a democracy, not as a technocracy run by puppet-masters. The hope of European republicans is to mobilize the political energy of pro-European youth and jump-start a pan-European movement. But the idea of a European Republic that strives to mobilize younger, cosmopolitan-minded Europeans has few chances today to have a political impact.

Why the democratization of public life and the emergence of an increasingly cosmopolitan younger generation fail to translate into support of Europe is at the nub of the West European paradox. It is enough to look at the Brexit vote and see that age and education were among the major factors defining how people voted. The younger and better educated were the core of the "remain" vote. After the financial crisis of 2008, it became clear that younger people had become politicized and empowered through social and other media. Political protests against the austerity policies favored by Brussels were an everyday experience in most European capitals. There exists a younger generation that speaks foreign languages, values the freedom to live and work anywhere in the EU, and is prepared to fight for fairness and justice. It is also a networked generation driven by social media. Knowing the ideological make-up and the political potential of this generation, it is natural to expect the emergence of a pan-European movement that would confront a Europe of elites with a Europe of citizens. Why then did such a movement never arise?

In trying to understand the failure of the connected generation to cross national boundaries and build an effective political movement in support of a stronger EU, it is worth reflecting on the findings of Zeynep Tufekci, one of the most insightful analysts of the politics of social media. Tufekci opened a recent talk at MIT's Media Lab with a photograph of the Hillary Step just below the summit of Mount Everest. Taken on a day that four people perished on the mountain, the picture shows the massive crowding that makes Everest perilous for climbers as they are forced to wait for others to finish before room opens up on the narrow trail.

Because of new technology and the use of Sherpas, more and more people who aren't expert climbers are streaming to Everest. Full-service trips (for a cool $65,000) get you to the base camp and much of the way up the mountain. But the guides still cannot adequately prepare people to climb to the peak. People have proposed fixing a ladder at the Hillary Step, standing at almost nine thousand meters above sea level, to reduce the risk. But the fundamental problem isn't the absence of a ladder; it's the exceptional difficulty of hiking at such a high altitude. The mountaineering community has suggested a reasonable solution: requiring people to climb seven other high peaks before they take on Everest.

This is Tufekci's analogy for Internet-enabled activism. In discussing the Internet and collective action, political commentators usually focus on the increased opportunities for coordination and community building. But in Tufekci's view, the wonders of the Internet are also a curse for the building of effective political movements. Social movements, like inexperienced mountaineers getting to base camp without adequately acclimating to exceptionally high altitude, show how some of the Internet's benefits can have significant handicaps as side effects. The result is that we are seeing increasing numbers of movements, but they may not have impact or endurance because they come to the public's attention too early in their lifetimes. Movements get stuck at saying "no," she argues, because they've never needed to develop a capacity for representation and can only coalesce around the negative rather than building an affirmative agenda.

My own work on protest movements supports Tufekci's conclusions. Fascinated by spontaneity and dreaming of a politics of horizontal networks, the new social movements, whether Indignados, Occupy, or one of the other antiausterity groups in Europe, succeeded for a period in demonstrating the power of citizens to resist. But they failed to have lasting political impact. The anti-institutional culture of the protesters and their rejection of any specific ideology doomed them to irrelevance. You may be able to spark a revolution with a tweet, but you can't tweet a government into power. (Even Donald Trump needed some help from the Republican Party apparatus.) What these protest movements will be remembered for are videos, not manifestos; happenings, not speeches; and conspiracy theories, not political tracts. They are a form of participation without representation. It is thus hardly accidental that the only two important political parties that came out of the antiausterity youth movements—Syriza in Greece and Podemos in Spain—only slightly resemble the horizontal dreams of the protesters. Both are traditional in their political organization, and their successes have been heavily dependent on the popularity of their respective leaders, Alexis Tsipras and Pablo Iglesias.

What seems clear are a series of aporias. The protesting citizen wants change but resents any form of political representation. Basing his theory of social change on ad copy from Silicon Valley, he values disruption and scoffs at political blueprints. He longs for political community but refuses to be led by others. He will risk clashing with the police but is afraid to risk trusting any party or politician. Mary Kaldor of the London School of Economics, who has been researching the new social movements in Europe, explains that although these movements have a transnational identity and protesters from different countries are in constant contact with each other, the idea of Europe and the reality of the European Union were almost entirely absent from the passions and interests of activists on the streets. Spontaneity tends to be local.

The idea of democracy without representation makes any serious discussion of the future of the European Union nearly impossible. A united Europe cannot exist without representation. But the uncompromising, anti-institutional ethos of young pro-EU activists makes a united Europe impossible. More disturbing still is that the political mobilization of pro-EU youth has led to the emergence of parties like Syriza and Podemos that strongly link the idea of democracy to the idea of national sovereignty. Although comprised of pro-EU youth, these parties often build their legitimacy on opposing Brussels. The fact that pro-Europeans perceive them as youth parties thus becomes a vulnerability for three reasons. First, young voters are a shrinking minority in Europe. Second, even when they are passionate about politics, young people are not in the habit of showing up to vote. And third, the support of younger people makes liberal politicians believe that the problems they face today will disappear once older generations die off. This is a grave delusion.

The Brussels Paradox

"I am persona non grata in my own country, with many blaming me for the crisis we are in and for their personal difficulties," writes a bitter George Papaconstantinou, the former Greek finance minister in his memoirs.[17] "I was the one who, when the music stopped, turned on the lights and told everyone the party is over . . . As a result, I have lived for years under a peculiar sort of 'house arrest.' Walking the streets became a dangerous sport." Papaconstantinou is not one of the corrupt Greek politicians who have robbed the country blind for decades. Neither is he a superrich fellow who converted his political power into money. Nor is he a member of one of the elite Greek political families who has run the country for the last century. He is simply one of Europe's model meritocrats who comes from an ordinary family, got a good education, and rose in the ranks of Greek society. He was invited to join the government of George Papandreou not really because of his ideological commitments but because of his competence and integrity. And yet he ended up one of the most hated men in Greece.

Why are Papaconstantinou and other meritocratic strivers from throughout the continent so resented at a time when the complexity of the world suggests their expertise and professionalism are needed more than ever? Why do people who work hard to send their kids to the world's finest universities refuse to trust people who are graduates from these very universities? How can it possibly be true that, as pro-Brexit politician Michael Gove put it, people "have had enough of experts"?

It is fashionable these days to discuss the crisis of the EU in terms of either the union's democratic deficit or its cosmopolitan makeup. But what's really at its core is the crisis of a meritocratic vision of society. This is demonstrated nowhere better than in the growing mistrust in meritocratic elites. Whether it's possible to have elites that are legitimate both at home and abroad is the pivotal question on which the European project hinges. We need to understand why meritocrats are so mistrusted, even though they are far from being the richest or the most corrupt people around.

It seems obvious that a meritocracy—a system in which the most talented and capable people are placed in leading positions—is preferable to a plutocracy, gerontocracy, aristocracy, and perhaps even democracy (the rule of the majority). But what we are witnessing today is a nonconfidence vote exactly against this vision of society.

Europe's meritocratic elites aren't hated simply because of the bigoted stupidity of raging populists or the confusion of ordinary people. Michael Young, the British sociologist who in the middle of the last century coined the term "meritocracy," would not be surprised by the turn of events.[18] He was the first to explain that even though "meritocracy" might sound good to most people, a meritocratic society would be a disaster. It would create a society of selfish and arrogant winners and angry and desperate losers. It will be not an unequal society but a society in which inequality is justified on the basis of differences in achievement. The triumph of meritocracy, Young understood, would lead to a loss of political community.

When analysts examine the Brexit vote in retrospect, they often agree that one of the key bottom-up drivers that determined the outcome was "a slow but relentless shift in the structure and attitudes of the electorate, the growing dominance of the middle classes, and of socially liberal university graduates."[19] In the 1960s, more than half of those with jobs in Britain did manual work, and less than 10 percent of the electorate had a university degree. By the 2000s, the working class had dwindled to around one-fifth of the employed electorate, while more than a third of the voters were graduates. Suddenly nobody was really interested in the working class. Blue-collar workers didn't lose their political importance, to be sure, but they started to be seen by analysts as groups of limited research interest. Meanwhile, the dramatic increase in the number of university graduates, who tend to be quite liberal, created a cultural gap between them and the remaining working class. Migration was the issue on which the two Britains clashed. Instead of being an instrument for creating more social cohesion, as progressives hoped a century ago, education has turned to be a cause of disunity.

What makes meritocrats so insufferable, especially in the minds of those who don't come out on top in the socioeconomic competition, is less their academic credentials than their insistence that they have succeeded because they worked harder than others, were more qualified, and passed exams that others failed.

In Europe, the meritocratic elite is a mercenary elite whose members behave not unlike soccer stars who get traded among the most successful clubs across the continent. They perfectly fit David Goodhart's definition of "people from Anywhere." Successful Dutch bankers move to London. Competent German bureaucrats head to Brussels. European institutions and banks, like soccer clubs, spend colossal amounts of money acquiring the best "players."

But when these teams start to lose or the economy slows, their fans soon abandon them. Principally, that's because there are no human relationships connecting the "players" and their fans beyond mutual celebration of victory. They're not from the same neighborhood, and they don't have mutual friends or shared memories. Many of the players aren't even from the same countries as their teams. You can admire the hired "stars," but you have no rational reason to feel sorry for them. In the eyes of the meritocratic elites, their success outside of their countries is evidence of their talent. But in the eyes of many, this very mobility is a reason not to trust them.

People develop trust in their leaders not only because of their competence, courage, and commitment but also because they sense that at a time of crisis, their leaders will hunker down and help out rather than rushing for the nearest emergency exit. Paradoxically, it is the "convertible competencies" of the present elites, the fact that they are equally fit to run a bank in Bulgaria or in Bangladesh or to teach in Athens or Tokyo, that makes people so suspicious of them. People fear that in times of trouble, the meritocrats will opt to leave instead of sharing the cost of staying. In this sense, meritocratic elites contrast with land-owning aristocratic elites, who are devoted to their estates and cannot take their estates with them in case they want to run away. They also contrast with communist elites, who always had better goods, better health care, and better education. But what they did not have was the power to leave; it was always easier for an ordinary person to emigrate. Communist elites, Princeton historian Stephen Kotkin has shown, were "no exit" elites, while meritocratic elites from the time of globalization and European integration are "no loyalty" elites.

Traditional aristocratic elites had duties and responsibilities and were reared to fulfill them. The fact that generations of their forebears, staring at them from portraits on the walls of their castles, had once themselves performed these same duties meant they took them seriously. In Britain, for example, the proportion of young men from the upper class who died in the First World War was greater than the proportion of the lower classes. The new elites, by contrast, are trained to govern, but they are not taught to sacrifice. Their children never died (nor even fought) in any war. The nature and convertibility of the new elites makes them practically independent of their own nations. They are not dependent on their country's education system (their children go to private schools) or the National Health Service (they can afford better hospitals). They have lost the ability to share the passions of their communities. People experience this independence of the elites as a loss of citizen power. Meritocratic elites are very connected, but their networks are horizontal. The leading economist in Sofia, Bulgaria, is intimately familiar with his colleagues in Sweden but has no knowledge of or interest in his compatriots who failed their technocratic examinations. He highly doubts he can learn anything from them.

Unsurprisingly then, it is loyalty—namely, the unconditional loyalty to ethnic, religious, or social groups—that is at the heart of the appeal of Europe's new populism. Populists promise people not to judge them solely on their merits. They promise solidarity if not justice. While meritocratic elites envision society as a school populated by "A" students who fight for fellowships against dropouts who fight on the streets, populists endorse a vision of society as a family where members support each other not simply because everyone deserves it but because everyone shares something in common.

At the very heart of the populist challenge is the struggle over the nature and obligations of elites. Unlike a century ago, today's insurgent leaders aren't interested in nationalizing industries. Instead, they promise to nationalize their elites. They don't promise to save the people but to stay with them. They promise to reestablish the national and ideological constraints that were removed by globalization. They praise the people for not speaking foreign languages and for having nowhere to go. In short, what populists promise their voters is not competence but intimacy. They promise to reestablish the bond between the elites and the people. And a rapidly increasing number in Europe today find this promise appealing.

The American philosopher John Rawls spoke for many liberals when he argued that being a loser in a meritocratic society was not as painful as being a loser in an openly unjust society. In his conception, the fairness of the game would reconcile people with failure. Today it looks as if the great philosopher may have been wrong.

The crisis of meritocratic elites at least partially explains the crisis of leadership in Europe. The frequently heard call for "leadership" has two very different meanings depending on where it is uttered. In Brussels and in many national capitals, the demand for leadership connotes resistance to populist pressure and courage to implement the most rational and effective policies. In these places where the elites of the continent congregate, it refers to a test that should be passed with the right answers. These elites view the political crisis of the EU mainly as a communications crisis in which Brussels has simply failed to explain its policies effectively.

But in the deindustrialized and depressed parts of the continent, the demand for leadership means something very different: a demand for sacrifice and loyalty. People expect leaders to declare their personal readiness to underwrite the cost of the crisis and to publicly exhibit their family obligations to their societies. From this standpoint, the crisis of the European project at bottom isn't so much the product of a democratic deficit as a demand for the meritocratic vision of society to be reimagined. Unfortunately for Europe, the clash between meritocratic elites and the populists has taken the form of political clash between the Exit Party and the Loyalty Party. It is not by accident that more often than at any other moment in the last fifty years, generals are in fashion not only in Russia but also in the West. One need only look to the composition of Donald Trump's administration in order to see that the populist promise is a government of generals who know how to defend their countries and business executives who are addicted to ruthless decisions.

Destroyed by Referendums

The electorate is "a sovereign whose vocabulary is limited to two words: 'Yes' and 'No,'" wrote the American political scientist, E. E. Schattschneider. He is basically right. Citizens tend to believe that only by saying "no," and much more rarely, "yes," their voices will be heard by the ruling class. And so when support for traditional political parties has plummeted and the confidence in democratic institutions is in question, many believe that a move to some form of direct democracy is the avenue to reform the democratic system.

The question of the legitimacy of referendums is one of democracy's oldest debates. Advocates of direct democracy argue that they are the most reasonable and transparent way for citizens to influence public policies beyond electing a government. In their view, referendums produce clear mandates (something elections generally can't do), stimulate public debate, and educate people, thereby achieving the democratic dream of a society of informed citizens.

The opponents of direct democracy disagree. They insist that referendums are not the best way to empower people but the most perverse way to manipulate them. In the words of Margaret Thatcher, referendums are a device of "dictators and demagogues." They dangerously simplify complex policy issues and often lead to incoherent policies because referendums look at issues in isolation, the result being that people may approve measures that contradict each other. It is generally believed that if citizens are going to be asked on the same day to vote for an increase in social spending and on tax cuts, they may likely support both (while politicians know full well that cutting taxes will make it impossible to increase social spending). The critics of direct democracy also argue that referendums are most often run by emotions and not by arguments. They deny that referendums foster civic engagement. The evidence bears this out. As referendums have proliferated, the median turnout for nationwide referendums across Europe has fallen from 71 percent in the early 1990s to 41 percent in the past few years.

What follows is not an argument about the advantages and disadvantages of direct democracy. What I argue, instead, is that in a political construction like the EU, where you have a lot of common policies, you have far fewer common politics. Where nobody can prevent member states voting on issues that can dramatically affect other states in the union, an explosion of national referendums is the fastest way to make the union ungovernable. Such an explosion could even trigger a "bank run" that could catalyze the breakup of the union. Europe can't exist as a union of referendums because the EU is a space for negotiation while referendums are the final word of the people that preclude further negotiations. Referendums are therefore political instruments that can be easily misused by both Euroskeptical minorities and euro-pessimistic governments to block the work of the union. If the EU commits suicide, the weapon used will quite likely be a popular referendum or a series of popular referendums.

A harsh shock can turn the unthinkable into the inevitable with frightening speed. This is precisely what happened in Europe after Britons voted to leave the union. The shock was particularly painful because European and British elites had managed to convince themselves that the "remain" camp would prevail. Experts, pollsters, markets—almost everybody predicted that the United Kingdom would stay in the union. Political oddsmakers gave Remain an astounding 93 percent chance of victory in the minutes before the first results were announced. All predictions turned out to be wrong, of course, and everything changed overnight.

The vote in favor of Brexit sent shockwaves around the world, rocking financial markets, frightening political leaders, and provoking far-reaching political debates. If the day before Brexit Europeans were arguing about which would be the next country to join the EU, the day after Brexit the question was who would next leave. In psychology, there is a well-known experiment in which a person is asked quickly to look at drawings of cats and is constantly asked what he or she sees. Unsurprisingly, he or she sees cats. Then the drawings of cats are mixed with occasional drawings of dogs, yet the person insists that he or she sees only cats. Soon somebody shouts a person's name distracting him or her from the drawings. When the person looks at them again, he or she starts to see the dogs. This is what happened with Europe on the night of

Chapter 2

June 23, 2016, the day the Brits voted to leave. It finally became possible to perceive the dogs.

Historians are quick to recall that referendums accompanied the two fateful disintegrations Europe witnessed in the last decade of the twentieth century: the shattering of the Soviet Union and the violent implosion of Tito's Yugoslavia. Referendums in the Yugoslav Republics put in motion what would become the collapse of Tito's federation; and in the Soviet Union, in paradoxical fashion, the March 1991 referendum conducted in nine of the Soviet Republics and resulting in a massive victory for the pro-union camp contributed to the collapse of the Soviet state. The vote demonstrated that national republics were the centers of political life in the union and that the USSR was sick and dying. The lesson was that a referendum could inspire disintegration even if majorities voted against it.

The crucial point here is that although pessimists are right to fear that the European Union will be destroyed by referendums, they are afraid of the wrong referendums. While in the wake of Brexit, we witnessed a growing desire among Europeans for binary-like "in-out" referendums, opinion polls indicate that with the passing of time the desire for such a final say has declined in most European countries. The likelihood of classical "in-out" referendums is quite limited in the vast majority of the member states. This can certainly change, but for the moment, the appeal of such referendums has declined. Pro-European elites will scarcely risk triggering the "nuclear option" after experiencing what transpired in Britain. Call this one the "Cameron effect." Moreover, what is common to all referendums that took place in 2016 is that governments never achieved their objectives. Populists, it is fair to say, prefer to threaten a stay or leave referendum than genuinely to advance one. After all, they have witnessed with Brexit the problems a successful anti-EU referendum invites. Their preferred strategy will likely be to insist that every election be an informal referendum on the EU rather than explicitly asking for an up-or-down vote on exit.

Rather than fixating on a Brexit-type referendum, we need to focus on three other referendums that took place in 2016. In the manner of Sergio Leone's classic spaghetti Western, let's call them the Brave, the Mean, and the Ugly. The Brave was former Italian Prime Minister Matteo Renzi's December referendum in Italy; the Mean, the Dutch referendum on the Ukrainian Association Treaty with the EU in April; and the Ugly, Viktor Orbán's October referendum on the refugee policy of the EU. These three referendums illustrate better than anything else the risk of the EU's breakup unfolding as a kind of a traffic accident.

The Brave

It should be no surprise that in the spring of 2016, Matteo Renzi hatched the idea of a referendum. Five years after the financial markets and the high command of Brussels succeeded in ejecting Silvio Berlusconi from power, Italy remained one of the main victims of the EU crisis. The Italian economy was in a kind of permanent stagnation with its banks particularly vulnerable. The Italian political system remained as polarized as ever, ineffective, and now marked by the rise of the eccentric Five Star Movement of political protest. At the same time, the country had become the portal through which most refugees and immigrants arrived to Europe. After the closing of the Balkan route in 2016, Italy became the epicenter of Europe's migration crisis. Compounding the distress, Matteo Renzi had become Italy's prime minister without having had to face the voters. It's hardly surprising that in a country where political issues are often decided through referendums, the young, new prime minister would be tempted to gamble, using the vote as a way to achieve popular legitimacy as well as support for a reform of the political system that would issue in a more effective decision-making process. The reluctance of Italy's opposition parties to support Renzi's reform package in the Parliament and the Senate made a referendum inevitable.

The questions Renzi put before the Italian people were loaded: "Do you approve the text of the Constitutional Law on 'Provisions for exceeding the equal bicameralism, reducing the number of MPs, the containment of operating costs of the institutions, the suppression of the CNEL, and the revision of Title V of Part II of the Constitution'?" Renzi had multiple objectives: reducing the power of the second chamber of parliament—the Senate, which is currently equal to the Chamber of Deputies—and thereby reforming the dysfunctional Italian "vetocracy," cutting the number of Senators from 315 to 100 and stripping the Senate of the right to hold votes of "no confidence" in the government, and ending direct elections of the Senate, populating it instead with twenty-one regional mayors, seventy-four regional council heads, and five members selected by the president. The proposed reforms would reduce the powers of Italy's twenty regional governments, handing over authority to the central government on such issues as energy, infrastructure, and foreign trade. Reformists say this would cut the cost of politics by half-a-billion euros per annum and expedite lawmaking by ending decades of parliamentary ping-pong. If the referendum had succeeded, it would have ended the system of "perfect bicameralism," thus giving more power to the government and enabling faster passage of legislation. Opinion polls before the vote suggested that the prime minister's chances of success were good and that the referendum would help position him as a rebel against the status quo, forcing his opponents to defend the existing political mess. In the words of Renzi himself, the reform was a battle between "nostalgia and the future, between those who want to change nothing and those who are looking ahead."[20]

On December 4, 2016, more than 65 percent of the electorate voted; 59 percent voted "no" and almost 41 percent "yes." Renzi's constitutional reform proposal was decisively defeated, and he was forced to resign. Analysts have speculated that it was the prime minister's own promise to step down in the event of a loss that transformed the vote from an evaluation of the electoral system to a judgment on the ambitions of a contested prime minister. However, we can only speculate how the results would have differed in the absence of Renzi's pledge.

On the day of the vote, Italy resembled a patient who, facing the date of his surgery, decides to bolt out of the hospital. The government's defeat made markets even more skeptical about Italy's capacity to deal with the crisis. It weakened Italy's position in negotiation with Brussels, and it boosted euro-pessimism among citizens across the continent. In the words of Marine Le Pen of France's far-right National Front, "After the Greek referendum, after Brexit, this Italian No adds a new people to the list of those who would like to turn their backs on absurd European policies that are plunging the continent into poverty."[21]

Renzi's failure on the referendum makes one thing clear. In the context of the current European crisis, when citizens have lost trust in democratic institutions and governments are viewed as enemies of the people, any attempt to use referendums as a way to mobilize support for reforms is most likely to be self-defeating. It may be true that the government or parliament has the authority to introduce a referendum question, but it is the people who get to decide what question they will answer.

The Mean

In 2015, the Dutch Parliament adopted a new referendum law that permits citizens to call for a consultative public vote on bills that have passed through both houses of Parliament. It requires three hundred thousand citizens to trigger an "advisory referendum" on laws and treaties of a "controversial nature." In the words of Gerard Schouw, a member of Parliament from the D66 Party, the referendum initiative was a way to regain the confidence of citizens. As Schouw notes, "This law will give citizens a serious opportunity to express their views and an important voice in the decision-making process."[22] The escalating antielite, anti-EU sentiments in Dutch society provoked mainly by citizen opposition to migration and the enlargement of the European Union made it inevitable that mainstream political parties would look for ways to demonstrate their readiness to listen to the people's concerns. Yet what ultimately occurred is that the new initiative not so much gives a voice to the people as it amplifies the noise produced by the Euroskeptic wing of Dutch society.

Exploiting the opportunity created by the new legislation, a group of Euroskeptical organizations began gathering signatures. They succeeded in gathering enough of them—more than 420,000—to organize a referendum in answer to the question: "Are you for or against the Approval Act of the Association Agreement between the European Union and Ukraine?" Turnout for the vote was a meager 32 percent of eligible voters, with 61 percent of those casting a ballot rejecting the agreement. Although the referendum was advisory and nonbinding, the fact that the turnout exceeded 30 percent (though just barely) and that a majority voted against it gave the results apparent legitimacy. Never mind that the referendum was devoted to an issue of essentially no interest to the vast majority of citizens. (Who would deny that outside of the government nary a soul read the entire two-thousand-plus pages of the treaty?) The outcome nonetheless compelled the government to revisit its position and placed into question the EU's fragile consensus on Ukraine.

In the words of one commentator, "The decision to focus on the association agreement between the EU and Ukraine was not oriented against the agreement as such, but rather against what they [GeenPeil—a provocative Dutch weblog] perceive as a lack of influence for Dutch voters within the EU." It may sound perverse, but the referendum was called as a useful occasion for mobilizing the Euroskeptic vote on an issue of no major consequence for those who support the union.

Once we grasp that the referendum was primarily about engaging Euroskeptics, it becomes easy to understand why the governing parties responded to it with such passivity. They feared that public opinion was in a "no" mood, so they pinned their hopes on turnout failing to reach the thirty-percent threshold. The leading parties were also afraid to lobby openly in favor of boycotting the referendum because doing so would contradict the claim that the new legislation instituting referendums was meant to permit the people to speak their minds. "The genius of [the referendum]," wrote Euroskeptical Amsterdam professor Ewald Engelton, "is that it has no consequence; the treaty will be ratified anyway. It is a crystal clear popularity poll: for or against the [political] caste—that is the question."[23] The sad conclusion is that the Dutch referendum was a powerful demonstration of how votes can be hijacked by Euroskeptical minorities and used tactically to paralyze the process of collective decision making in Brussels by pushing pro-European governments to rally for issues that are of no interest to the public.

The Ugly

A foreigner visiting Hungary in the summer and autumn of 2016 could not miss a series of government-installed billboards posted throughout the country, all of them colored the same blue as the EU flag and posing the question: "Did you know?"

The anti-immigrant gambit of the ruling Fidesz Party issued in a massive PR campaign. Citizens were confronted by thousands of government-sponsored billboards asking: "Did you know that since the beginning of the immigration crisis, more than 300 people have died as a result of terror attacks in Europe?" "Did you know that Brussels wants to settle a whole city's worth of illegal immigrants in Hungary?" "Did you know that since the beginning of the immigration crisis the harassment of women has risen sharply in Europe?" "Did you know that the Parisian terror attacks were committed by immigrants?" "Did you know that close to one million immigrants want to come to Europe from Libya alone?" The government wanted Hungarian citizens to be aware of these "facts" when on October 2, they were asked to answer the question, "Do you want the European Union to be able to order the mandatory settlement of non-Hungarian citizens in Hungary without parliament's consent?"

By defending the idea of a referendum on the EU refugee policy, Hungarian prime minister Viktor Orbán insisted that

> first of all, we are convinced that the path which the Hungarian government has chosen to follow—the path leading to a referendum—is a European solution; it is a feature of European politics, and therefore we wholeheartedly recommend it to others also. The Government believes that democracy is one of Europe's core values, and the European Union is also based on the foundations of democracy. This means that we may not adopt decisions—those that significantly change people's lives and also determine the lives of future generations—over the heads of the people, and against the will of the European people. The quotas would redraw the ethnic, cultural, and religious map of Hungary and of Europe. The Hungarian government takes the view that neither the EU, nor Brussels, nor the leaders

of Europe have the authority to do this; in fact, there is no European body or agency of any kind that has been vested with such authority. To date no one has asked the European people whether they want, accept, or reject the introduction of compulsory quotas. We Hungarians believe—and I am convinced that the government was yielding to the general desire of the public when it chose to call a referendum—that introducing compulsory re-settlement quotas without the consent of the people is nothing less than an abuse of power. Therefore we shall ask the people of Hungary about this question, just as we asked about Hungary's accession to the European Union. . . . No one but us, the elected representatives of the Hungarian parliament, can make this decision.[24]

To grasp the motives behind Orbán's referendum, it's necessary is to recognize that the government decided to ask people to vote on one of the few issues on which there was consensus in Hungarian society—opposition to Brussels's decision to settle refugees in different EU countries. The government didn't ask people to vote because it was interested in their opinions; it pressed people to vote because it *knew* their opinions. The referendum that took place in Hungary on October 2, 2016, was really meant as a message to Brussels. By organizing the referendum, Prime Minister Orbán hoped to achieve three simple objectives: to demonstrate to the public that he is the real defender of the nation's interests and thus to marginalize the support for the extreme right-wing Jobbik Party with whom he competes for the nationalists' vote, to signal to Brussels that Hungary will remain firm in rejecting a European quota system for the refugee crisis, and to show the citizens of Europe that the Hungarian prime minister is the true leader of a new conservative Europe that will defend national borders and fight to transfer power from Brussels to national capitals.

To achieve its objectives, the Hungarian government spent nearly fifty million euros of public money (according to atlatszo.hu), and Hungarian public TV devoted 95 percent of campaign time restating the government's position. By comparison, the money spent on Brexit by the UK government in support of both the Leave and Remain campaign was roughly seven million euros less. In the end, the Hungarian government spent €5.00 per person on its single-sided campaign, while the Brits spent only €0.66 per person on theirs. The government also sent more than four million full-color booklets to Hungarians at home and abroad making the government's case for why Hungarians should vote "no" on the EU's refugee policy. The irony is that the government was in a position to spend so lavishly precisely because of billions of euros coming into the country from . . . Brussels.

The results of the referendum came as a shock to the government. While more than 90 percent of those who voted supported the government's position, the majority of people opted to stay home (as prompted by the opposition) or voted with invalid ballots (there were two hundred thousand of those). The Two-Tailed Dog Party, a group of pranksters that together with twenty-two NGOs became the government's chief opponent over the course of the campaign, may have had the last laugh: the number of ballots cast was insufficient to validate the results.

Despite the inconclusive outcome in this case, the Hungarian vote demonstrates how referendums can be used as a "national veto" to stymie the implementation of agreed-upon, common European policies. Along with the votes in Italy and the Netherlands, it illustrates Europe's potentially fatal referendum conundrum. The crisis of liberal democracy in EU member states is a product of the widely shared feeling, significantly worsened since the financial crisis of 2008, that the votes of individuals have no meaning or effect on European policy. Forced to address this sensation of impotence, political elites have tried to bolster the legitimacy of the political system by introducing an element of direct democracy. Yet that element of direct democracy may well end up sinking the European Union.

As Renzi's poll clearly demonstrates, the referendum is an unreliable instrument when institutional reform is the desired end. The Dutch case makes clear how it can be used to paralyze the union. And the Orbán vote shows how a referendum can be deployed to advance explicitly anti-Brussels ends. All three kinds of referendums have the power to shape the EU's political dynamics and to empower a form of outright euro-pessimism that goes far beyond the Euroskepticism of recent years.

Perhapsburg—Reflections on the Fragility and Resilience of Europe

"Man tends to regard the order he lives in as natural," wrote Czesław Miłosz in a now distant 1951.

> The houses he passes on his way to work seem more like rocks rising out of the earth than like products of human hands. He does the work he does in his office or factory as essential to the harmonious functioning of the world. . . . He cannot believe that one day a rider may appear on a street he knows well, where cats sleep and children play, and start catching passers-by with his lasso. In a word, he behaves a little like Charlie Chaplin in *The Golden Rush*, bustling about in a shack poised precariously on the edge of a cliff.[1]

For Europeans, the European Union was such a natural world. It is not anymore. The year 1917 was one that turned European history on its head. It started the great civil war in Europe that ended only in 1989. The year 2017 may end up being just as consequential. Pivotal elections in the Netherlands, France, Germany, and most likely Italy, may escalate the process of European disintegration. Greece may opt to leave the eurozone in 2017. Major terrorist attacks in a European capital, or armed conflict and a new wave of refugees on Europe's periphery, could easily bring the union to the edge of collapse. Brexit and the election of Donald Trump have upended future predictions of Europe's survival—and not in Europe's favor. If the disintegration of the EU was only recently considered unthinkable, after Brexit it seems (in the eyes of many) almost inevitable. Europe has been shattered by the rise of populist parties across the continent, just as the migration crisis has transformed the nature of liberal democratic regimes.

Democracy in Europe, which had long been an instrument for inclusion, is now slowly being transformed into a tool for exclusion. The minority-friendly regimes of the early post–Cold War period are being supplanted by majoritarian regimes that are openly intolerant and anti-pluralistic. The dream (now fantasy) of a Europe without frontiers is being replaced by the grim reality of a barricaded continent.

In many corners of Europe, there is a growing anxiety that the populist wave cannot be reversed. On the day Donald Trump took his oath as president of the United States, the leader of the French Far Right Marine Le Pen proclaimed, "The European Union is dead, but it does not know it yet."

But is this true?

It may be fair to say that the European Union (as we have known it) no longer exists. The smart money is betting against the EU. And even EU-friendly analysts tend to agree that if the union is going to survive, it will do so neither in its current borders nor with its current constitutional framework. But does that mean that the European project is over? Should pro-European liberals surrender their hopes?

At this point, déjà vu mind-set returns to teach a powerful lesson. Having once witnessed a major historical reversal, one knows that historical determinism is an illusion—opium for people on the edge of a nervous breakdown.

Machiavelli insisted that surrender is a bad idea because we never know what surprises fortune may have in store for us. In Machiavelli's view, there are "good times" and "bad times" in politics, and the good ruler is not one who can fend off the "bad times" so much as one who has accumulated enough goodwill among citizens to help him ride out those bad times.

The argument of this short book is that European Union is going through a really bad time today, torn apart by numerous crises that damage confidence in the future of the project among citizens across the continent. So the disintegration of the union is one of the most likely outcomes.

Yet, paradoxically, 2017 comes with a renewed source of hope that was lacking in 2016. No one expected the outcome of the Brexit vote or the American presidential election. The shock inspired by these twin events sends us a message that we do not understand the world as well as we thought we did. In 2017, we therefore face a very different dynamic. We are not only aware that the unthinkable can happen, but we actually expect it to happen. We fear but also expect that Geert Wilders will be the big winner of the Dutch elections, that Marine Le Pen will end up as the new president of France (which would probably spell the end of the EU), and that Merkel's moment in German politics has come to an end. All this really may happen, but most likely it will not. Wilders already has lost an election in the Netherland. And while populist parties will probably do well, they will not triumph everywhere. Post-Brexit, the number of people in major EU member states who want their countries to leave the union has declined. It's quite possible that European publics will become more confident about the EU not because it's become better but simply because it has survived.

In reality, the union's various crises, much more so than any of Brussels's "cohesion policies," have contributed to the sense that we Europeans are all part of the same political community. In responding to the euro crisis, the refugee question, and the growing threat of terrorism, Europe has ended up more integrated than ever before, at least when it comes to economics and security.

The close study of the history of political disintegration reveals that the art of survival is an art of constant improvisation. Flexibility—not rigidity—is what may yet save Europe. While most observers ask how populism can be vanquished, in my view the more apposite question is how to respond to its venality. What will increase the likelihood of the European Union surviving is the spirit of compromise. Making room for conciliation should be the major priority of those who care for the union. The EU should not try to defeat its numerous enemies but try to exhaust them, along the way adopting some of their policies (including the demand for well-protected external borders) and even some of their attitudes (free trade is not necessarily a win-win game). Progress is linear only in bad history textbooks.

It's less important that European leaders understand why the Habsburg Empire collapsed in 1918 than why it did not disintegrate earlier, in 1848, 1867, or on any number of other occasions. Rather than seeking to ensure the EU's survival by increasing its legitimacy, perhaps demonstrating its capacity to survive can become a major source of its future legitimacy.

It's often said that Europe is endangered by its lack of visionary leaders. But do we honestly know what kind of leaders would be able to save the union?

In his book *The Anatomy of a Moment*, Spanish writer Javier Cercas tells the story of the failed antidemocratic coup in Spain in 1981.[2] It was the most decisive moment in recent Spanish history. People were still fearful of the power of the old regime and already disappointed in their early experiences with democracy. Unemployment sat at 20 percent, and inflation was approaching 16 percent. Talk of a coup was in the air. Everybody expected something to happen. Finally, two hundred officers of the Civil Guard led by Lieutenant Colonel Antonio Tejero entered the legislature and threatened to shoot members of parliament. Everyone flung themselves under the benches except for three people who remained in their seats while bullets whizzed around them. With their stunning display of courage, they doomed the coup to failure.

The three heroes of democracy were the most unlikely bedfellows: Prime Minister Adolfo Suarez, a politician who made his career during Franco's dictatorship;

Santiago Carrillo, the leader of the Spanish Communist Party, who for years had been railing against the injustices of capitalist democracy; and General Gutierrez Mellado, an officer who risked his life in the Civil War fighting against democracy. Before that fateful day, no one would have predicted that these three would face down the putschists and thereby ensure the survival of democracy in Spain. But it happened.

Survival is a little like writing a poem: not even the poet knows how it's going to end before it does.

Notes

Introduction

1. Joseph Roth, *The Radetzky March* (London: Granta Books, 2003).

2. Oszkar Jaszi, *The Dissolution of the Habsburg Monarchy* (ACLS Humanities e-book, 2009), 4.

3. Jan Zielonka, *Is the EU Doomed?* (Cambridge: Polity Press, 2014).

4. José Saramago, *The Stone Raft* (New York: Mariner Books, 1996).

5. Walter Laqueur, ed., *Soviet Union 2000: Reform or Revolution* (New York: St. Martin's Press, 1990), xi.

6. Francis Fukuyama, "The End of History?," in *The National Interest*, Summer 1989.

7. Mark Leonard, *Why Europe Will Run the 21st Century* (London: Fourth Estate, 2005), 11.

8. Ivan Krastev and Mark Leonard, "Europe's Shattered Dream of Order," *Foreign Affairs*, May/June 2015.

9. Benjamin F. Martin, *France in 1938* (Baton Rouge: Louisiana State University Press, 2005), 1.

10. Alexei Yurchak, *Everything Was Forever, Until It Was No More: The Last Soviet Generation* (Princeton: Princeton University Press, 2005), 1.

11. Mary Elise Sarotte, *Collapse* (New York: Basic Books, 2014), xix.

12. Mark Lilla, *The Shipwrecked Mind: On Political Reaction* (New York: New York Review Books, 2016).

Chapter 1

1. José Saramago, *Death with Interruptions* (Boston: Houghton Mifflin Harcourt, 2005).

2. Francis Fukuyama, "The End of History?," in *The National Interest*, Summer 1989.

3. Ken Jowitt, "After Leninism: The New World Disorder," *Journal of Democracy* 2 (Winter 1991): 11–20. Jowitt later elaborated his ideas in *The New World Disorder: The Leninist Extinction* (Berkeley: University of California Press, 1992); see esp. chapters 7–9.

4. Ibid., 310.

5. Francis Fukuyama, "The End of History?," in *The National Interest*, Summer 1989.

6. Harry Kreisler interview with Ken Jowitt, "Doing Political Theory," Conversations with History, Institute of International Studies, UC Berkeley (Regents of the University of California, 2000). http://globetrotter.berkeley.edu/people/Jowitt/jowitt-con5.html.

7. Ibid.

8. Jamie Bartlett, Jonathan Birdwell and Mark Littler, *The New Face of Digital Populism* (London: Demos, Magdalen House, 2011) https://www.demos.co.uk/files/Demos_OSIPOP_Book-web_03.pdf.

9. Convention and Protocol Relating to the Status of Refugees (Public Information Section: 1996, UNHCR / PI / CONV-UK1.PM5 / AUGUST 1996), 16. http://unhcr.org.ua/files/Convention-EN.pdf.

10. Michel Houellebecq, *Submission: A Novel* (New York: Farrar, Straus and Giroux, 2015).

11. Karl Ove Knausgaard, "Michel Houellebecq's 'Submission,'" *New York Times*, November 2, 2015. https://www.nytimes.com/2015/11/08/books/review/michel-houellebecqs-submission.html.

12. Gaspar Miklos Tamas, "What Is Post-fascism?," *openDemocracy.net* 13 (September 2001). https://www.opendemocracy.net/people-newright/article_306.jsp.

13. Ayelet Shachar, *The Birthright Lottery: Citizenship and Global Inequality* (Cambridge, MA: Harvard University Press, 2009).

14. Slavoj Žižek, "The Cologne Attacks Were an Obscene Version of Carnival," *New Statesman* 13 (January 2016).

15. "History of the World Values Survey Association," http://www.worldvaluessurvey.org/WVSContents.jsp?CMSID=History.

16. Raymond Aron, *The Dawn of Universal History: Selected Essays from a Witness to the Twentieth Century* (New York: Basic Books, 2002).

17. Slavoj Žižek, "We Can't Address the EU Refugee Crisis without Confronting Global Capitalism," *In These Times*, September 9, 2015. http://inthesetimes.com/article/18385/slavoj-zizek-european-refugee -crisis-and-global-capitalism.

18. David Goodhart, *The Road to Somewhere: The Populist Revolt and the Future of Politics* (London: C. Hurst, 2017).

19. Stephen Holmes, *The Cost of Rights: Why Liberty Depends* (New York: W. W. Norton, 2000).

20. Kelly M. Greenhill, "The Weaponisation of Migration," in *Connectivity Wars*, ed. Mark Leonard (London: European Council on Foreign Relations, 2016), 77.

21. Edward Luttwak, "Why Fascism Is the Wave of the Future," *London Review of Books* 16, no. 7 (April 7, 1994). https://www.lrb.co.uk/ v16/n07/edward-luttwak/why-fascism-is-the-wave-of-the-future.

22. Samuel P. Huntington, *Who Are We?: The Challenges to America's National Identity* (New York: Simon & Schuster, 2004), 21.

23. Karen Stenner, *The Authoritarian Dynamic* (Cambridge: Cambridge University Press, 2005).

24. Jonathan Haidt, "When and Why Nationalism Beats Globalism," *The American Interest* 12, no. 1 (July 10, 2016). http://www.the-american -interest.com/2016/07/10/when-and-why-nationalism-beats-globalism/.

25. Matthew Smith, "People across the West Think We Are Close to a New World War," *YouGov Research*, January 5, 2017. https://today .yougov.com/news/2017/01/05/people-major-western-nations-think -world-close-maj/.

26. Patrick Donahue and Arne Delfs, "German President Backs Refugee Limits in Challenge to Merkel," *Bloomberg.com*, January 20, 2016. https://www.bloomberg.com/news/articles/2016-01-20/german-president -backs-refugee-limits-as-path-to-public-support.

27. Bertolt Brecht, "Das Lied von der Unzulänglichkeit des menschlichen Strebens," 1928. http://www.lyrikline.org/en/poems/ballade-von -der-unzulaenglichkeit-menschlichen-planens-770#.WNUJbNKLTcs.

28. Paul Collier, *Exodus: How Migration Is Changing Our World* (Oxford: Oxford University Press, 2015).

29. Zero G Sound, July 29, 2016. https://zerosounds.blogspot.bg/ 2014/01/wolf-biermann-das-geht-sein.html?m=0.

30. Fundamental Rights Report 2016, European Union Agency for Fundamental Rights. http://fra.europa.eu/en/publication/2016/fundamental-rights-report-2016.

31. Pew Research Center, July 2016, "Europeans Fear Wave of Refugees Will Mean More Terrorism, Fewer Jobs," Global Attitude Survey, Spring 2016. http://assets.pewresearch.org/wp-content/uploads/sites/2/2016/07/Pew-Research-Center-EU-Refugees-and-National-Identity-Report-FINAL-July-11-2016.pdf.

32. Henry Foy, "Poland's New Majoritarians," *The American Interest* 12 (June 7, 2016). http://www.the-american-interest.com/2016/06/07/polands-new-majoritarians/.

33. Tony Judt, *A Grand Illusion?: An Essay on Europe* (New York: NYU Press, 2011), 57.

Chapter 2

1. Timothy Garton Ash, "Is Europe Disintegrating?," *The New York Review of Books*, January 19, 2017.

2. *Special Eurobarometer 379*, 2012, http://ec.europa.eu/public_opinion/archives/ebs/ebs_379_en.pdf.

3. Roberto Stefan Foa and Yascha Mounk, "The Democratic Disconnect," *Journal of Democracy* 27, no. 3 (July 2016): 5–17, 7.

4. Ibid., 10.

5. David Remnick, "An American Tragedy," *The New Yorker*, November 9, 2016, http://www.newyorker.com/news/news-desk/an-american-tragedy-2.

6. Dani Rodrik, *The Globalization Paradox: Democracy and the Future of the World Economy* (New York: W. W. Norton, 2012).

7. Walter Bagehot, *The English Constitution*, 2nd ed. (1873), 61.

8. James Dawson and Sean Hanley, "Has Liberalism Gone Missing in East Central Europe, or Has It Always Been Absent?," *Open Democracy*, October 5, 2015.

9. Viktor Orbán's speech at Băile Tuşnad (Tusnádfürdő) of 26 July 2014, http://budapestbeacon.com/public-policy/full-text-of-viktor-orbans-speech-at-baile-tusnad-tusnadfurdo-of-26-july-2014/10592.

10. Jan-Werner Müller, *What Is Populism?* (Philadelphia: University of Pennsylvania Press, 2016), 3.

11. Philip Bump, "Donald Trump's Spectacular, Unending, Utterly Baffling, Often-Wrong Campaign Launch," *The Washington Post*, June 16, 2015. https://www.washingtonpost.com/news/the-fix/wp/2015/06/16/donald-trumps-spectacular-unending-utterly-baffling-often-wrong-campaign-announcement/?utm_term=.aac10285ae5b.

12. Rob Brotherton, *Suspicious Minds: Why We Believe Conspiracy Theories* (London: Bloomsbury, 2015), 6.

13. Smolensk Crash News Digest is focused on issues surrounding the April 10, 2010 crash of Polish government Tupolev Tu-154M, near Smolensk, Russia. http://www.smolenskcrashnews.com/.

14. Maria Szonert Binienda, "Smoleńsk Maze: Crash of the Polish Air Force One, Smoleńsk, Russia, April 10, 2010," Status Report 2014, Libra Institute (Cleveland: Libra Institute, 2014), 3. http://www.smolenskcrashnews.com/pdf/2014_Report/2014_Smolensk_Status_Report.pdf.

15. Ibid., 21.

16. "Big Brother Gives Politics Lesson," *BBC News*, June 3, 2003. http://news.bbc.co.uk/2/hi/uk_news/politics/2956336.stm.

17. George Papaconstantinou, *Game Over: The Inside Story of the Greek Crisis* (Athens: Papadopoulos, 2016), 10.

18. Michael Young, *The Rise of the Meritocracy 1870–2033: An Essay on Education and Society* (London: Thames and Hudson, 1958).

19. Robert Ford and Matthew Goodwin, "Britain After Brexit: A Nation Divided," *Journal of Democracy* 28 (January 2017): 17–30.

20. "Italy Referendum 'Is a Choice between Nostalgia and the Future,'" *The Local*, November 7, 2016. https://www.thelocal.it/20161107/italy-referendum-is-a-choice-between-nostalgia-and-the-future.

21. "Italian Referendum Result Is Unhelpful for EU, but Not a Fatal Blow," *The Guardian*, December 5, 2016. https://www.theguardian.com/world/2016/dec/05/italian-referendum-result-eu-eurosceptics-far-right-austria-matteo-renzi.

22. "Over 440,000 Dutch Call for Referendum on Ukraine EU Treaty," *DutchNews*, September 27, 2015. http://www.dutchnews.nl/news/archives/2015/09/over-440000-dutch-call-for-referendum-on-ukraine-eu-treaty/.

23. Simon Otjes, "Could the Netherlands' Referendum on Ukraine Really Create a 'Continental Crisis'?" http://blogs.lse.ac.uk/europpblog/2016/01/26/could-the-netherlands-referendum-on-ukraine-really-create-a-continental-crisis/.

24. Prime minister Viktor Orbán's press conference, February 24, 2016. http://www.kormany.hu/en/the-prime-minister/the-prime-minister-s-speeches/prime-minister-viktor-orban-s-press-conference.

Conclusion

1. Czesław Miłosz, *The Captive Mind* (New York: Vintage; reissue edition, 1990).

2. Javier Cercas, *The Anatomy of a Moment*, translated by Anne McLean (London: Bloomsbury, 2011).

A c k n o w l e d g m e n t s

It sometimes feels as if it would be easier to document the hundreds of thousands of refugees and migrants who came to Europe in 2016 than to name all the people who have influenced this book and the institutions from whose generosity I have benefited.

The true shaper of this book was Lenny Benardo, who twice read and edited it. His insights can be found on many pages. A number of the ideas I articulate here grow out of conversations with Stephen Holmes and Mark Leonard. Jan-Werner Müller and John Palattella not only read and commented on the book in detail but did much to shape my thinking about populism. Soli Ozel and Fyodor Lukyanov offered me important insights on Turkey and Russia. I am indebted to Damon Linker, my editor at Penn Press, and to my literary agent Toby Mundy for their persistent critical encouragement. Toby was great in making me believe that there is only one thing worse than writing a book in the middle of a great transformation: not to write it at all.

I would like to thank my colleagues at the Center for Liberal Strategies in Sofia, Bulgaria, and particularly

Yana Papazova, for their unconditional support and help. Without Yana, this book would never have been finished. IWM provided me with abundant time and ideal working conditions. I also benefited enormously from discussions and lunchtime exchanges with many IWM fellows, but I would like to single out Holly Case and Shalini Randeria. Holly is as passionate about the EU as only an American historian of nineteenth-century Europe could be, and Shalini is as knowledgeable about Europe as one might expect from an Indian intellectual who has spent his entire career on the continent. I was privileged two years ago to be offered the chance to write a monthly column for the *New York Times*. The regularity of this exercise has disciplined my mind, while my editors, Clay Risen and Max Strasser, have helped me to do a better job of capturing what is really important in current debate. Marc Plattner of the *Journal of Democracy* allowed me to explore the book's themes in his pages and, in doing so, allowed me to benefit from his editorial suggestion. To Adam Garfinkel, I owe the literary neologism "Perhapsburg." This word alone prompted me to see Europe through a different set of analytical eyes.

I would like to thank my family, with whom I practice the daily routine of reflecting on developments around the world: my wife, Dessy, who is a master of the art of civil disagreement and an adept at posing questions nobody else dares to ask; and my daughter, Niya, and son, Yoto, whose very existence urges me on in seeking understanding of the world they will grow up to live and thrive in.